What others are saying about the ministry of Tom Brown:

"Each week Pastor Tom Brown delivers dozens of souls from Satan's grip."

—The History Channel TV

"Sunday morning, El Paso, Texas, demons are cast out of repentant believers."

—*20/20*, ABC TV

"Tom Brown is out in front, battling Satan, leading the charge against an evil that appears to have so many souls in torment and looking for deliverance."

—MSNBC *Investigates* TV

"If anyone is a specialist on deliverance, Tom Brown surely is. This book breaks new ground and clearly shows the reader how to be free. Read it and get ready to experience the power of God and live the victorious, overcoming life that the Lord intended for you."

—Dennis Tinerino, Prophet/Evangelist
Dennis Tinerino Ministries
Mr. America
Four-time Mr. Universe

"The book is excellent. I appreciate the biblical perspective regarding the demonic and how to effectively deal with the challenges we Christians have with this unseen realm."

—Willard Thiessen, host of *It's a New Day*

"Despite the prevailing attitude of modern culture, the devil and demons are real! Tom Brown brings fresh and helpful insights on how to deal with these beings through spiritual warfare. His book is not only firmly founded in biblical truth, but is also written from working experience in helping countless people get free from the destructive activity of demons. This is a must-read book for any person who is serious about understanding the often misunderstood realm of the demonic. I know Tom Brown to be a person of integrity; he is a man who knows what he is talking about, and I recommend this book!"

—Pastor Brandon Honeycutt
All Nations Church, San Antonio, TX

"If you want to be free and want to put the devil in his proper place (which is under your feet!), then this book is for you. I enjoyed reading this book and I know you will too. You will find, as I did, that you'll want to read it again to dissect it and absorb the truth revealed within. A powerful book. I highly recommend it."

—Jesse Duplantis, Evangelist and television minister

"After spending many years in ministry dealing with spiritual matters such as demonic forces, I found Tom's book scriptural and helpful in giving new insights to this important subject. Jesus told us cast out demons in Mark 15:17, and this book shares effective, dynamic, principles that we all can apply on a daily basis."

—Don Gossett, Evangelist and Best-selling author

DEVIL
DEMONS
AND
SPIRITUAL
WARFARE

Power to Engage and Defeat Demonic Forces

TOM BROWN

WHITAKER
HOUSE

Devil, Demons, and Spiritual Warfare:
Power to Engage and Defeat Demonic Forces

Tom Brown Ministries
P.O. Box 27275
El Paso, TX 79926
www.tbm.org

ISBN: 978-1-60374-072-2
Printed in the United States of America
© 2008 by Tom Brown

Whitaker House
1030 Hunt Valley Circle
New Kensington, PA 15068
www.whitakerhouse.com

Library of Congress Cataloging-in-Publication Data
Brown, Tom, 1963–
  Devil, demons, and spiritual warfare / Tom Brown.
     p. cm.
  Summary: "Tom Brown argues that the Christian church has forgotten that it shares the mission of Jesus Christ: to engage in spiritual warfare in order to defeat the adversary of this world, Satan and his demons" —Provided by publisher.
  ISBN 978-1-60374-072-2 (trade pbk. : alk. paper) 1. Devil—Christianity. 2. Spiritual warfare. I. Title.
  BT982.B76 2008
  235.4—dc22   2008029531

4 5 6 7 8 9 10 11 **WH** 15 14 13 12 11 10

Acknowledgments

First of all, I want to thank my powerful Lord for setting me free and enabling me to help others gain their freedom.

Sonia, I thank you for standing by my side for twenty-five years as my soul mate.

My gratitude goes out to two wonderful women who proofread the book and offered invaluable suggestions: Anne Amaro and Gail Walsh.

Finally, I thank the members of Word of Life Church, who first received the message of this book and convinced me that many others could be helped through the word God gave me.

Contents

Introduction:

Freedom for the Whole Family

The television producers of *Judge Judy* and *Crossing Over with John Edwards* contacted me to ask if I would be interested in hosting my own reality TV show on the subject of exorcism. Even though I told them I was not ready for such a task, I am more than ready to help you find your freedom and victory in Christ.

I'm not like the many people who discount the reality of the devil and demons or who have suggested that it is all in your head! Like many of you, I have faced the devil and his power. I know what it is to sense him breathing down my neck. I know the feelings of powerlessness over his works, but I have also broken through to victory, and so can you. By God's grace, I have been used in freeing others from demons.

Cindy is one example. She was a young mother who came forward in one of my meetings. When I went to pray for her, she ran away, holding her baby in her arms. Others were about to block the exit to stop her from leaving, but I told them, "Let her go, if that's what she wants." Just then, Cindy froze in the doorway, looking at me and then at the exit. I told her, "Come down here and let me pray for you. You don't want to stay like this, do you?" After about a minute, she walked slowly toward me, and one of our leaders gently took the baby from her arms for safekeeping.

After giving Cindy a prophetic word, I spoke directly to the demons within her and told them to leave. She let out a high-pitched scream and fell to the floor. When she arose, Cindy was completely free from her demons.

I asked, "Have you ever made Jesus Lord of your life?"

She shook her head.

"Would you like to accept Christ now?"

With a smile, she nodded yes.

As I was about to lead her to Christ, a young man came forward to stand next to her. He was her husband, and he, too, wanted to accept Christ. As I was about to lead them both to the Lord, an older man walked forward to stand next to them.

"I'm her father. I want to get saved, too."

As I led them in prayer, that whole family was saved and delivered in a single night.

I believe this book can bring deliverance to you and your whole family. Cindy's problems were similar to many others'—depression, suicidal thoughts, anger, and obsessions. Perhaps, like Cindy, the devil has descended on you with feelings of condemnation. Perhaps demons are saying, "You are too far gone to be helped." Or, perhaps they have enslaved you with addictions too strong to overcome in your own strength. Perhaps their grip is so tight that you fear for your very life.

Hold on! Help is on the way.

In your hands is a book that can bring freedom for you and your loved ones. Don't give up. God has an answer for you.

What You Will Learn

In this book, I have attempted to present sound teachings, both scriptural and rational, about the devil, his demons, and your deliverance. I hope what you learn will provide the answers you need to be free and fulfilled. In addition,

+ you will learn why an understanding of Satan is so important.

+ you will discover what keeps people from seeing the light.

+ you will uncover Satan's plot against you.

+ you will recognize the need to accept forgiveness to keep Satan away from you.

+ you will be able to tell whether or not you need deliverance.

+ you will be instructed how to cast out demons.

+ you will find the answer to the question: Can Christians have demons?

+ you will guard yourself from going overboard on the practice of deliverance.

+ you will be strengthened to take charge over the battleground of your mind.

How the Book Is Arranged

This volume is divided into three sections. The first section deals with the lead general of the forces of evil: Satan. You will learn his number-one strategy and how to overcome it.

In the second section, you will be equipped with the knowledge you need to cast out demons.

The third section deals with fallen angels. This part is extremely important, for it shows how fallen angels work to create an atmosphere to help demons to carry out their diabolical work.

This book is unabashedly Christian in its approach. I do not make any apologies for believing that *"there is no other name under heaven given to men by which we must be saved"* (Acts 4:12). Others may debate the Bible's inspiration, but I simply use it as the Word of God to set captives free. If you are looking for a book that takes spiritual warfare seriously, while maintaining a biblically balanced approach, then this book is for you!

Part One

The Devil

Chapter One

The Villain

Filmmaking has always interested me. Recently, I became curious about how to write a good screenplay. In my research, I came across a successful screenwriter who offered this sound advice: the plan of the hero is not as important as the plot of the villain.

Something about those words struck a chord with me. He was explaining that unless the story has a strong villain, no one will care about the potential hero.

Superman is a great example. Would anyone really care about Superman's powers or his love for Lois Lane if he were not forced to battle the diabolical Lex Luther? Would Batman be as compelling without the Joker? Would Luke Skywalker's quest matter as much without Darth Vader? Would Clarice seem so brave without the opposition of Hannibal Lecter? In other words, great heroes are only heroic when facing great villains. Without such strong opposition, the greatness of their character would remain unknown to us.

The concept of hero and villain is not just for the silver screen. It is also true in real life. For example, Winston

Churchill is considered one of the greatest heroes in history, not necessarily for his political or economic theories, or his brilliant mind and oratorical skills, but because he went to war against Adolf Hitler. Few would remember Churchill's name today if his strong leadership had not been at his nation's helm during the historic conflict of World War II.

The greatest story ever told is the tale of God's response to the plot of His enemy, Satan.

Whether we realize it or not, the concept of hero and villain is played out in the spiritual universe, as well. The greatest story ever told is the tale of God's response to the plot of His enemy, Satan. The gospel is God's response to Satan's schemes. It is the demonstration of God's love for mankind—a love that caused Him to risk everything to rescue us from the hands of Satan.

Satan's plan was to separate Adam and Eve from God by tempting them to disobey His Word and eating from *"the tree of the knowledge of good and evil"* (Genesis 2:17).

Reason for the Incarnation

The intention behind Satan's plot was to usurp the authority God had given mankind. When God created man, He gave him dominion over all of creation, saying, *"Be fruitful and increase in number; fill the earth and subdue it. Rule over the fish of the sea and the birds of the air and over every living creature that moves on the ground"* (Genesis 1:28). Through Satan's plot, however, he was able to render the first couple's dominion over him null and void. Not only were Adam and Eve not able to rule the serpent, but the serpent became ruler over them.

God's plan, therefore, had to go beyond merely forgiving sinners—it also had to include reestablishing their dominion over Satan.

Consider the words of the apostle John: *"The reason the Son of God appeared was to destroy the devil's work"* (1 John 3:8). The word *reason* indicates a purpose. It demonstrates God's real motive: to defeat and conquer the devil, once and for all. Most Christians do not consider Satan's defeat as at the core of Jesus' incarnation. John, however, considered it the very reason for His coming.

It is my great concern that the body of Christ is leaving out this essential purpose for the gospel. Some think Christianity would be better served if the concept of the devil was removed completely from our message. On the contrary, I believe the church is better served by reintroducing the plot of our villain. Only then will we appreciate God as our great hero.

Rescued from Darkness

Someone might ask, "Isn't the gospel about God satisfying His own sense of justice? What does that have to do with defeating the devil?" Of course, the gospel is about God forgiving us; however, that forgiveness is possible only when we are rescued from the grip of the darkness that threatens to keep us from turning away from sin and seeking His forgiveness.

> *For he has rescued us from the dominion of darkness and brought us into the kingdom of the Son he loves, in whom we have redemption, the forgiveness of sins.* (Colossians 1:13–14)

Salvation is nothing less than God rescuing us from Satan's dark grip. Only then are we able to see the truth: that we have been aligned with the devil through *sin*, but because of Christ's sacrifice for our *sins*, our connection with the devil has been broken.

Once you understand Satan's role in keeping people in darkness, you will come to appreciate the specific and urgent need to cast demons out of people's lives. Demons are Satan's "ground troops" whose main job is to keep people in darkness. Demons succeed at doing this by binding people with terrible sins and circumstances until their situations seems to be greater than God's power to forgive and redeem.

To combat the work of demons, Jesus gave a clear commission to His church, not just to the original twelve apostles: *"And these signs will accompany those who believe: In my name they will drive out demons"* (Mark 16:17). Some Christians balk at this order, but it must be carried out.

To make this order clear, Jesus, after His ascension, gave a postscript commission to the apostle Paul:

> *I am sending you to them to open their eyes and turn them from darkness to light, and from the power of Satan to God, so that they may receive forgiveness of sins and a place among those who are sanctified by faith in me.* (Acts 26:17–18)

These were not Jesus' final words *before* He ascended on high, but rather, they are the command He gave to the apostle Paul *after* His ascension. It is very clear: *"turn them from darkness to light, and from the power of Satan to God."* Unfortunately, the world is blissfully unaware that Satan is ruling them by his power. As believers in the gospel, we are ordered to free people from Satan's powerful hold so they can *"receive forgiveness of sins."* The only reason people remain in their sin is because of the dark force that keeps them ignorant of the truth.

The only reason people remain in their sin is because of the dark force that keeps them ignorant of the truth.

Saving My Grandfather

Being from a broken home, I was raised by my grandparents. My grandfather was an atheist—not a sophisticated one, but an atheist nevertheless. I told him everything I knew about God and Jesus, which wasn't much at the time, but I shared it with all the sincerity I could muster.

He argued back, "I don't believe there is a God in heaven. You see this chair? This is god. And you see this table? It's god, too. This world is the only god I know."

I pleaded with him, "Grandpa, you're wrong. There is a God in heaven, and He loves you so much that He sent His only begotten Son, Jesus Christ, to save you, so that you can have eternal life with Him in heaven."

"I don't believe in Jesus Christ. He was just a man like us."

Those words crushed me. I couldn't understand how my grandpa could be so wrong and not see who Jesus really is.

One day, as I was praying for God to save my grandpa, the Lord spoke to me, saying, "Tom, you keep asking Me to save your grandpa, as if you need to talk Me into it. I want him to become saved. The problem is not with Me. I'm not willing that any should perish. (See 2 Peter 3:9.) The problem is with the devil."

In that moment, the Lord taught me about the role Satan plays in keeping people from being converted. He first led me to read in 2 Corinthians,

> *Satan, the god of this evil world, has blinded the minds of those who don't believe, so they are unable to see the glorious light of the Good News that is shining upon them. They don't understand the message we preach about the glory of Christ, who is the exact likeness of God.*

> (2 Corinthians 4:4 NLT)

It is not that they do not *want* to see the light; they are *unable* to see it. You cannot be angry at a blind man for not appreciating the color of a rainbow any more than you can get angry at a sinner who cannot appreciate the glorious light of God's grace through Christ. The sinner is *"blinded."*

On that day, the Lord seemed to say to me, "Satan is the god of all unbelievers. It doesn't do much good to ask Me to save unbelievers, because I'm not their personal God. Yes,

I'm the God of all mankind, but I'm not necessarily their Lord and Savior. (See Romans 10:9–10.) Now, you can ask Me to send forth laborers into the harvest field. (See Matthew 9:38.) The laborers are My children and I can instruct them on what to do, but I will not force unbelievers to accept Me—it must be their choice. What good would it do for Me to order unbelievers to accept Me if no one is witnessing to them? Instead, ask Me to send people to cross their paths so they can hear the gospel."

So, I asked God to send people to my grandfather. When I did, the Lord seemed to say, "Okay, I'm sending *you*. You're the laborer for your grandfather."

"But Lord," I said, "I have been witnessing to him; he doesn't seem to respond."

The Lord responded, "If your grandfather understood the gospel, he would love to get saved. Unfortunately, the god of this age has blinded his mind from comprehending it."

"What do I do, then?"

"I have given you My authority and power to bind the devil from blinding your grandfather's mind. Say out loud to him, 'I bind you, devil, from blinding my grandfather's mind! Stop it now, in Jesus' name!'"

"Are you telling me that the only reason why my grandfather hasn't gotten saved is because the devil has blinded his mind?"

"Yes."

"You must give me another Scripture to prove this."

The Lord took me to the parable of the sower. He made me study the people along the path who heard the Word: *"Those along the path are the ones who hear, and then the devil comes and takes away the word from their hearts, so that they may not believe and be saved"* (Luke 8:12).

The Lord asked me, "Why did those people along the path not believe and get saved?"

We have the same authority as Paul! We can turn people from the power of Satan by binding his efforts and by preaching the gospel to them.

I looked carefully, and then I saw it. The Bible says that *"the devil comes and takes away the word from their hearts."* The reason that they did not believe was because the devil stole the Word from them.

"That's right! Many of My people think that unbelievers don't get saved because they choose not to be saved. In truth, many unbelievers would choose to be saved if the devil did not steal the Word from their hearts. So stop the devil from stealing the Word by *binding him.* Bind him with your words! Tell him to stop! Because of the authority I've given you, he'll have to obey you."

Just as Paul was commissioned and given authority to *"open their eyes and turn them from darkness to light, and from the power of Satan to God"* (Acts 26:18), I took this commission personally. We have the same authority as Paul! We can turn people from the power of Satan by binding his efforts and by preaching the gospel to them.

Once the Lord showed me this truth, I walked into my grandfather's bedroom and said, "Grandpa, I realize that you would want to get saved if you understood the gospel. The devil is the one blinding your mind, so I'm going to bind him from your life right now."

There in his bedroom, I shouted at the devil and told him to leave my grandfather, who stood there, speechless. I left the room, confident that he would be saved. Immediately, there was a change in him. He finally confessed his belief in the existence of God, though he was still hesitant to accept Jesus as God's Son. Later, however, he began to talk much about God and Jesus in interchangeable terms.

My aunts asked me what I had done to Grandpa. "Tommy, all Grandpa wants to talk about is God—God this and God that. He doesn't stop talking about Him. He has never been concerned about any religious discussions, but now it's all he talks about." I smiled as I heard this. Grandpa was now seeing and feeling the warmth of God's great love for him.

Before long, I married my wife, Sonia. A few months into our marriage, the Lord led us to pray the prayer of agreement from Matthew for my grandfather to become saved.

> *Again, I tell you that if two of you on earth agree about anything you ask for, it will be done for you by my Father in heaven.* (Matthew 18:19)

On the following Monday, I was on my way to visit my grandfather, as usual. I drove to his house and walked into his bedroom with a big smile on my face. My grandfather was lying in bed, sick. I knelt beside his bed and said, "Grandpa, the Lord showed me that you're ready to get saved. Are you ready to get saved?"

Without hesitation, he nodded. "I'm ready." I led him in the sinner's prayer. We wept as we prayed together.

Soon after that, my wife and I started our first church. Although my grandfather was incapacitated because of his age, he asked my father to bring him to a service at my new church. I'll never forget it. My dad practically carried him in and sat him down on a chair in the back. As everyone stood up to sing to the Lord, my grandfather made the biggest effort to stand up, which he managed to do. With his left hand holding a chair in front of him for balance, he lifted his right hand to praise the Lord along with the rest of us.

That was the first and last service he was able to attend. His health continued to deteriorate until he died not so long after that. Now, my grandfather is in heaven, the real place full of happiness and joy! He is there, in part, because I understood there was a real battle for his soul. Can you imagine where my grandfather would be if I had not understood that we have a real villain?

Through this experience, the Lord taught me something that I will never forget. He seemed to be saying, "Remember, Tom, you are the answer to many people's prayers." Since that time, I've taken this responsibility seriously and have recognized the fact that, whether they know me or not, many Christians are counting on me to reach their loved ones for Christ. I am the laborer they have been praying for.

You, too, are the answer to people's prayers. Right now, people are praying for God to send laborers to go to their loved ones…and God has sent you.

Chapter Two

The Villain's Plot

"I *fear that somehow you will be led away from your pure and simple devotion to Christ, just as Eve was deceived by the serpent*" (2 Corinthians 11:3 NLT). Paul was not a man prone to fear. Yet something about the Corinthian church caused his heart to beat faster. What was his concern? He feared Satan was leading this congregation away from their pure and simple devotion to Christ.

Once again, this is the plot of Satan.

It has never changed. It was formulated during the time that God gave a simple command to Adam:

> *You are free to eat from any tree in the garden; but you must not eat from the tree of the knowledge of good and evil, for when you eat of it you will surely die.* (Genesis 2:16–17)

It was not hard to understand. "Don't eat from that one particular tree. Leave it alone." In order for Adam and Eve to show their true devotion to God, all they had to do was obey this simple command.

Enter the serpent. Make no mistake about it, the serpent is a pseudonym for the devil, for he is called the *"ancient serpent"* (Revelation 20:2). Shrewdly, he asked Eve, *"Did God really say, 'You must not eat from any tree in the garden'?"* (Genesis 3:1).

Eve replied, *"We may eat fruit from the trees in the garden, but God did say, 'You must not eat fruit from the tree that is in the middle of the garden, and you must not touch it, or you will die'"* (verses 2–3).

Obviously, Eve was already confused in her understanding. First, God had said nothing about *touching* the fruit, only that they were not to eat it. Second, the tree *"in the middle of the garden"* was the tree of life, and there was no command about eating from it. The command to Adam and Eve had been so simple; how could she be confused?

> *As long as you are unclear about what God says, you are primed for deception.*

This is the beginning of deception. As long as you are unclear about what God says, you are primed for deception. This is why I am greatly concerned for our society, because they are dangerously ignorant of the Bible.

The serpent, after questioning God's motives, said, *"You will not surely die....For God knows that when you eat of it your eyes will be opened, and you will be like God, knowing good and evil"* (verses 4–5). The serpent's logic seemed to rattle Eve. The serpent had put a thought into her head: *Why wouldn't God want me to be like Him?*

As Eve looked at the fruit, she became curious. She was also hungry. Another thought: *What better food could there be than this? It will feed my body and my mind at the same time. I will become wise like God. Just like Him, perhaps even equal to Him! After that, I might not even need Him anymore.*

Such thoughts of independence seemed all too wonderful to Eve. She had to have this fruit. She took some and ate it. Her husband, longing to share his wife's experience, also took the fruit and ate it. They were no longer devoted to God. The serpent had succeeded. His plot had worked!

Perfect in Wisdom

There is a good explanation for Satan's success. The Bible tells us that he was the only creature that God created as *"the model of perfection, full of wisdom"* (Ezekiel 28:12). His wisdom was perfect, and he was skilled in using it for any purpose. He was so skilled in using this wisdom that he convinced one-third of the angels to join his side and war against God. (See Revelation 12:4.) He was, and still is, very persuasive. The Bible says he *"corrupted* [his] *wisdom"* (Ezekiel 28:17), taking something good and God-given and perverting it for his own selfish purposes. He corrupted one-third of the angels to his side, and then he corrupted Adam and Eve, God's prized creation, as well.

The apostle Paul did not underestimate this opponent. He knew that the devil is so sly that he can make good appear evil and evil appear good. Paul was not just a tad concerned for his church; he was gravely distressed at Satan's work among the believers.

Even today, the alarm in heaven is being sounded! Wake up! The devil is alive and working. He is deceiving God's people. Make no mistake about it, he's *good*—not good in the moral sense, but very effective at what he does—at deceiving people.

The church landscape is filled with souls brought down because they believed Satan's lies—marriages are destroyed, churches are split, pastors are discouraged, families are torn apart, heresies are taught. I'm not referring only to what is happening in the world, but in our church pews, as well. People are hurting. They listen to the sermons, but they can't seem to move forward. They hear of God's love, but they don't understand why they fail to experience it. They hear about the power of prayer, but they wonder why their prayers seem to bounce impotently off the ceiling.

Rick was a wonderful minister whom God used magnificently to restore marriages. More than a hundred thousand divorces were cancelled by people who attended his seminars. He preached this message in more than twenty countries with outstanding results. The devil, however, knew that if he could ensnare Rick, many more would fall with him. Soon, he began to assault Rick with feelings of anger toward his wife. Rick began to believe that his wife did not esteem him in the way she should. On top of that, he soon met another woman who stroked his ego. He became convinced that this other woman was made for him. Even though Rick had always believed that the devil was behind divorces, when it came to his own marital breakup, Rick was blinded from realizing that the enemy of God was tempting him with this other woman. To the complete shock of the Christian community, Rick eventually divorced his wife to marry this woman.

Believe me, if Rick could fall, anyone can fall.

Unfortunately, few realize that they are in a real battle against the forces of darkness. They simply don't take Satan seriously. Either they don't believe he's real or they refuse to believe that he would specifically target them. Yet he does.

Ignorance Is Not Bliss

Lest Satan should get an advantage of us: for we are not ignorant of his devices.

(2 Corinthians 2:11 KJV)

Paul could not have written this to the church today, because, unfortunately, we are woefully ignorant of Satan's devices. Far too many believers are losing the battle with Satan because they are ignorant of his simple plot: to drag them away from their walks with God. He will use everything at his disposal to do this.

Sin is Satan's one real weapon. Deception is the means by which he will compel a person to sin.

Sin is Satan's one real weapon. Deception is the means by which he will compel a person to sin, and he will use it in an attempt to deceive you into sinning against God, as well.

Part of our problem is that we no longer regard *sin* as real. We have replaced the word with other more politically correct terms like *problems, weaknesses, human frailties,* and *mistakes.* Even so, our main problem is still sin. The Bible relates the word *sin* to our relationship with God. When we sin, we are breaking a command of God, known or unknown. Whether you know something is wrong is beside the point; if you do that which God commands you not to do, you have sinned. Some may ask, "What was so wrong about Adam and Eve eating from the tree of the knowledge of good and evil?" It was wrong for one reason: God commanded them not to do it. The issue was not about eating an apple, but about disobeying God.

Often, people will question whether something is wrong based on their *perception* of right and wrong instead of on whether God has declared something off-limits. If God says not to do something and you do it anyway, even if it is something you deem harmless, that is sin. You can argue about why it is acceptable, but if God says you cannot do it, then it is a sin to do it. You may believe that your happiness depends on doing something that is forbidden by God; your happiness, however, is not the core issue; your obedience is. Satan will go to any length to make disobedience seem attractive—he may even make it seem healthy—but he will never reveal the high price you will pay for your disobedience.

Satan convinced Eve that her life would be better if she ate the fruit. He not only told her that she would not die, but he also said she would become like God. Nothing Satan promised turned out to be true. Ultimately, she was banished from the garden, she experienced the pain of childbirth, and, eventually, she died. Satan will make all kinds of attractive promises to anyone who will listen, but, for the most part, he will not fulfill them.

The ultimate result of Adam and Eve's sin was death— not only "physical" death, but also "spiritual" death. Paul wrote,

> *You were dead in your transgressions and sins, in which you used to live when you followed the ways of this world and of the ruler of the kingdom of the air, the spirit who is now at work in those who are disobedient.* (Ephesians 2:1–2)

It's clear that death was not merely a physical one, for how could Paul write to a people who were physically dead? He must have been referring to a spiritual death. Spiritual death is separation from God. Paul also referred to this as being *"separated from the life of God"* (Ephesians 4:18).

God's life flowed through Adam and Eve in the garden. As long as they remained loyal to God, His life would be their life, and they would not taste death. After their rebellion, however, they were separated from that source of life. Although they would not die physically for many years, they died spiritually the moment they ate the fruit.

There is absolutely nothing God has for us that can be enjoyed while we are stubbornly disobeying Him.

This is Satan's goal for everyone. First, he wants to keep the sinner from ever receiving God's gift of eternal life. Second, even after salvation, Satan desires to keep the saints from truly experiencing abundant life. The only thing that will accomplish this is sin! Sin hurts our ability to walk in God's nature. We can't love while we are being selfish. We can't experience joy while we are miserably sinning. We can't experience peace while our consciences are nagged in the wake of our disobedience. There is absolutely nothing God has for us that can be enjoyed while we are stubbornly disobeying Him.

Pride, the First Sin

"God opposes the proud but gives grace to the humble." Submit yourselves, then, to God. Resist the devil, and he will flee from you.

(James 4:6–7)

Many Christians have attempted to stand on this verse, but they fail to receive its benefits because they do not practice the entire passage. Most will only quote the part that says, *"Resist the devil, and he will flee from you,"* then wonder why he does not flee. They have ignored the first part, which says, *"God opposes the proud but gives grace to the humble."*

God originally opposed Satan because of his pride. *"Your heart became proud on account of your beauty"* (Ezekiel 28:17). Pride was the original sin. It was not, however, committed by man, but by an angel. As it turns out, *"the devil has been sinning from the beginning"* (1 John 3:8). At his creation, man was innocent, and he lived for a while in that state of innocence.

Satan knows the Scripture that says, *"Pride goes before destruction, a haughty spirit before a fall"* (Proverbs 16:18). Pride always precedes sin; therefore, his first temptation is to get you to think more highly of yourself than you should.

During the Last Supper, a dispute arose among the disciples as to which one of them was to be the greatest. (See Luke 22:24.) Can you imagine that? Jesus was predicting His death, and all they could talk about was who would be in charge when He was gone. Jesus, hearing their discussion, said,

> *Simon, Simon, Satan has asked to sift you as wheat. But I have prayed for you, Simon, that your faith may not fail. And when you have turned back, strengthen your brothers.* (Luke 22:31–32)

Consider the audacity of the leader of heaven's rebellion asking Jesus for permission to attack Simon Peter. In fact, the Greek word *ask* actually means "to demand." What gave Satan such boldness to approach God in this manner? One thing: Peter had entered enemy territory—pride—giving Satan a legal right to make him suffer. I find no other sin in Scripture that gives Satan this right. Sinful pride, after all, originated with him. He corrupted it.

I find it interesting that Jesus did not address Peter by his newly given name of "Rock." Instead, He used the humble name, "Simon." He even used it twice—*"Simon, Simon"*—perhaps trying to remind Peter of his humble origins, urging him to keep his pride in check. Peter did not listen, though, but instead boasted, *"Lord, I am ready to go with you to prison and to death"* (Luke 22:33).

Not only was Peter far from ready to become a martyr, but he was also the only one of the twelve who, during Jesus' trial, actually denied even knowing Him. The others had the common sense to run away before they were put in such a position. Not Peter. He stayed near Christ, watching from a distance. Soon, a young girl asked him if he knew Jesus. Peter said, *"Woman, I don't know him"* (Luke 22:57). Later, someone else accused him of having been with Jesus. Peter quickly replied, *"Man, I am not!"* (verse 58). An hour later, another man recognized Peter as a Galilean, and announced that he must have been with Jesus. Peter, fearing the arrest and death he once boasted he could handle, insisted, *"Man, I don't know what you're talking about!"* (verse 60). At that moment, Scripture says that Jesus turned toward Peter and looked deeply into his eyes. Overwhelmed by his own betrayal and cowardice, Peter ran away weeping!

Jesus had predicted that Peter would do this, and yet He also had confidence in the disciple's repentance. That's why, at the Last Supper, He included the words, *"When you have turned back, strengthen your brothers"* (verse 32). In other words, "Peter, I am not giving up on you. You are not disqualified from leadership. You are still My man!"

Aren't you grateful for the Lord's mercy? What a great lesson about the deception of pride. Just when you think you will never fall—bam!—you are hit with an irresistible temptation. You are brought low and humbled by your complete failure. You have learned a painful lesson in the misleading power of pride.

As much as you try to resist Satan, if you are prideful, how will you make him flee? You are operating on his level.

God will not violate His Word and give you power over Satan if you are acting in pride. This is why so many fail to gain any power over Satan. Their hearts are infected with sinful pride. Not only can they not *"resist Satan,"* but according to Scripture, God *"opposes"* (James 4:6) them. You are not on God's side if you are prideful, for you have sided with the devil.

It's equally important that you do not fall for false humility, which always makes you feel as if you are unworthy to fulfill your calling. While Peter eventually expressed true humility and experienced God's mercy, Judas allowed his treacherous act to so infect his self-worth that he hanged himself out of guilt.

As long as you cannot accept forgiveness, you will not be able to rise up and fulfill your call.

As terrible as sin is, guilt is even worse. As long as you cannot accept forgiveness, you will not be able to rise up and fulfill your calling. Judas betrayed Christ but would not accept forgiveness. Satan convinced him that his betrayal would never be forgiven by God. In truth, it could have been, but he gave up before he could experience God's mercy. Peter, on the other hand, betrayed Christ but accepted God's forgiveness, and, in his humility, was restored into his place of leadership.

Chapter Three

Satan Is Disarmed

> *When you were dead in your sins and in the uncircumcision of your sinful nature, God made you alive with Christ. He forgave us all our sins, having canceled the written code, with its regulations, that was against us and that stood opposed to us; he took it away, nailing it to the cross. And **having disarmed the powers and authorities,** he made a public spectacle of them, triumphing over them by the cross.* (Colossians 2:13–15, emphasis added)

How was the cross able to disarm Satan? It's simple. Satan's primary weapon is *condemnation*—to condemn us for the sin he tempts us to do. Little did he know that God's plan was to take away our sins, thus depriving Satan of his primary weapon. *"None of the rulers of this age understood it, for if they had, they would not have crucified the Lord of glory"* (1 Corinthians 2:8).

Jesus had foretold Satan's predicament: *"When a strong man, fully armed, guards his own house, his possessions are safe. But when someone stronger attacks and overpowers him, he takes away the armor in which the man trusted and divides up the spoils"* (Luke 11:21–22).

In order to rob the devil of his possessions, Jesus first took away the armor in which he put his trust, then divided the spoils. In order for us to partake in the spoils—health, victory, and prosperity—Jesus had to remove sin from our lives, which kept us from righteousness and its rewards. The cross, therefore, dismisses Satan's legal indictment against us and brings us acquittal from our sins. Once acquitted, we then have legal rights to the plunder.

In the Old Testament, Satan made a very rare appearance, showing up at one point because Joshua, the high priest, had committed a gross sin. While it is true that Joshua was a symbol of the nation of Israel, there is nothing in the story to indicate that Joshua himself had not sinned. It is likely the writer used Joshua's personal—and very public—failure to illustrate Israel's own corporate failure, and ultimately God's great mercy for both. Of course, the incident also can be extended to apply to us and illustrate how Jesus took away our sin.

The story begins with the prophet Zechariah having a vision. In it, he saw Joshua standing next to the archangel, his head bowed in humiliation. He looked like a criminal awaiting sentencing before a judge. In the place of a bright orange prison jumpsuit, Joshua wore the filthiest of garments and was not prepared to defend himself.

Opposing him was Satan himself, a smirk across his face and a finger pointed toward the condemned Joshua. As he opened his mouth to begin the prosecution's case, however, the entire courtroom shook. Everyone was amazed as God's voice thundered and an angel interpreted, *"The LORD rebuke* you, Satan! The LORD, who has chosen Jerusalem, rebuke you! Is not this man a burning stick snatched from the fire?" (Zechariah 3:2).

What's happening? Satan must have wondered. *Wait a minute, God! It is Joshua who has disgraced his office. Let me tell you what he did!*

As God ignored him, the angel spoke to the rest of the assembly, *"Take off his filthy clothes"* (verse 4). Then, with great compassion, the angel said to Joshua, *"See, I have taken away your sin, and I will put rich garments on you"* (verse 4). Joshua was forgiven! The angels rejoiced! Israel was glad! Zechariah turned to the other priests and instructed them to place a clean turban on Joshua's head—he was restored to leadership. An even closer look at the story reveals what an important role *community* played in the restoration and forgiveness of Joshua. It was not enough that God forgave the sinner; the people of God also had to show forgiveness to him.

> *It was not enough that God forgave the sinner; the people of God also had to show forgiveness to him.*

A similar situation took place in the church at Corinth. One of the leaders had committed a horrible act. *"It is actually reported that there is sexual immorality among you, and of a kind that does not occur even among pagans: A man has his father's wife"* (1 Corinthians 5:1). The apostle Paul could not understand how this congregation could have ignored such an act. He commanded them to remove the man from the fellowship and hand him over to Satan. (See verse 5.)

In the next letter, Paul addressed the issue again; by this time, however, the offender felt great sorrow over what he had done and had repented. This sorrow worked repentance in his soul, yet the congregation felt that Paul would desire the man to remain excommunicated. Paul had to explain the need to forgive and restore the man, *"The punishment inflicted on him by the majority is sufficient for him. Now instead, you ought to forgive and comfort him, so that he will not be overwhelmed by excessive sorrow"* (2 Corinthians 2:6–7). Sorrow is good, but *"excessive sorrow"* can become a tool of the enemy. *"And what I have forgiven—if there was anything to forgive—I have forgiven in the sight of Christ for your sake, in order that Satan might not outwit us. For we are not unaware of his schemes"* (verses 10–11).

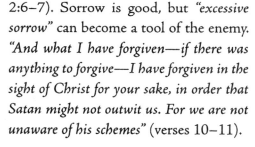

Far too often, the church is unwilling to offer forgiveness and restoration to those who have fallen—even after they have repented.

It is clear that Satan's scheme was to overwhelm the repentant man in Corinth with excessive sorrow. According to Paul, beyond the man's own repentance, the only way for him to experience healing and restoration was for the community to restore him. If they did not, Satan would have won the victory.

Far too often, the church is unwilling to offer forgiveness and restoration to those who have fallen—even after they have repented. They are quick to uphold God's standards of holiness but slow to uphold God's standards of love and mercy. We cannot continue to shun Christians who have stumbled and disappointed us. Whether it is a pastor, deacon, musician, Sunday school teacher, or any volunteer in the church, when someone makes a terrible blunder we cannot continue to deny him fellowship after he has truly repented. He must be restored.

This is why Joshua had to be restored as high priest. It was not enough for him to be placed as a lower priest. We are giving Satan the lead when we allow vengeance or anger to overrule restoration. These two examples from Scripture are great pictures of the need for the religious community to forgive and restore—as well as examples of Satan's defeat.

I once knew a pastor who had established a vibrant and successful ministry that had won hundreds of souls, built a large congregation, and showed promise of doing even more. He was a great teacher with a magnetic personality. Yet, like so many Christian leaders of our day, he succumbed to sexual temptation.

It looked like his ministry was over. One particular verse haunted him: *"As dead flies give perfume a bad smell, so a little folly outweighs wisdom and honor"* (Ecclesiastes 10:1). To me, it seemed unfair that all the good this man had done was to be forever outweighed by one act of indiscretion. He was fully intending to resign when a woman in the church had a dream. In the dream, this pastor was preaching effectively behind the pulpit, but he suddenly fell forward off the platform, landing in the seats of the congregation. The woman was excited about this dream, and she told the pastor, "God showed me that you fell forward, not backward." The dream encouraged this man to continue in the ministry. Through his repentance and his congregation's forgiveness and restoration, his ministry is bigger today than ever before.

He had learned the same important lesson that Joshua did: God forgives even great sin, but the sinner must believe this and put on the garments of a right standing with God. Being forgiven of a great sin can bring a new sense of gratefulness. For my pastor friend, this experience gave him a greater understanding and empathy toward the failures of his flock.

The Atonement

In the garden of Eden, Satan's hope was for Adam and Eve to sin. He succeeded; however, the last thing Satan wanted was for sin to be taken away. This is what the cross is all about.

The theological term is *atonement.* It means "to cover, to remove, to erase what once was there."

> God presented him [Christ] as a sacrifice of atonement, through faith in his blood. He did this to demonstrate his justice, because in his forbearance he had left the sins committed beforehand unpunished—he did it to demonstrate his justice at the present time, so as to be just and the one who justifies those who have faith in Jesus.
>
> (Romans 3:25–26)

In the Old Testament, God commanded Moses to establish a sacrificial system whereby innocent animals—lambs, bulls, goats, and the like—would die as an atonement for Israel's sins. A major feast called the Day of Atonement was established at the coming of the New Year. On this day, the high priest slaughtered two animals. One was killed for its blood; the other was sacrificed in the fire. A third animal, a goat, was not killed but was instead taken outside the city, where the priest laid his hands on it, confessing "onto it" all the sins of the Israelites. The goat—the scapegoat— was then released into the wilderness, never to be seen again. (See Leviticus 16:5–10.) What a great picture of sin being removed!

Being forgiven of a great sin can bring a new sense of gratefulness.

Satan watched this ceremony each and every year, but it must have never registered in his mind what it would eventually mean. Satan inspired the religious leaders to have Jesus crucified, not realizing that by doing so, Jesus would become the scapegoat—a supreme sacrifice that would remove sin from all of humanity.

In the garden of Eden, God foreshadowed *how* the seed of the woman would one day administer Satan's defeat. "*He will crush your head, and you will strike his heel*" (Genesis 3:15). Both parties would be wounded. The heel of the Messiah—from the woman's seed—would be bruised, but Satan's head would be crushed. Head injuries are usually much more fatal than foot injuries. God was warning creation that there was a price to be paid for administering Satan a fatal blow. That price would include death, "*for the wages of sin is death*" (Romans 6:23). Jesus paid the price that was due on our account. With the atonement completed, the only thing left was for the sinner to accept the pardon.

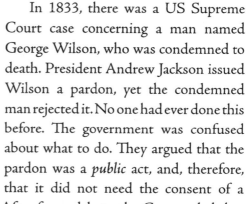

When Jesus paid the price that was due on our account the only thing left was for the sinner to accept the pardon.

In 1833, there was a US Supreme Court case concerning a man named George Wilson, who was condemned to death. President Andrew Jackson issued Wilson a pardon, yet the condemned man rejected it. No one had ever done this before. The government was confused about what to do. They argued that the pardon was a *public* act, and, therefore, that it did not need the consent of a *private* individual. After fierce debate, the Court ruled that although the pardon was a public act, it was intended for a private benefit, and therefore ruled that,

> A pardon is a deed, to the validity of which, delivery is essential, and delivery is not complete without acceptance. It may then be rejected by the person to whom it is tendered; and if it be rejected, we have discovered no power in a court to force it on him.

(UNITED STATES v. GEORGE WILSON 32 U.S. 150, 7 Pet. 150, 8 L.Ed. 640)

In other words, for a pardon to be effective, it must be accepted.

I bring this up because, while the price of your sin has been paid, it was a public act of grace before the world that was intended to bring private blessings. Thus, you must legally accept God's pardon, offered through the atonement, in order for it to be effective. The *atonement* is God's action; *acceptance* is your action. Beware, however, because Satan will do everything he can to keep you from accepting forgiveness.

Condemnation

> *Now have come the salvation and the power and the kingdom of our God, and the authority of his Christ. For the accuser of our brothers, who accuses them before our God day and night, has been hurled down. They overcame him by the blood of the Lamb and by the word of their testimony.*
> (Revelation 12:10–11)

The devil does not quit simply because we have received salvation. Notice in the passage above whom the devil is accusing—not the sinner, but *"our brothers."* The saint's greatest fight is to maintain a clear and good conscience. Forgiveness is granted to us by God; He cannot, however, grant us clear consciences.

Many people are forgiven by God but continue to struggle to maintain clear consciences. The devil does not help. He continuously tries to shame us with our pasts. He stands before God night and day, accusing us and hoping that God will somehow change His mind about us. Satan hopes that through his accusations he might cause us to hold on to feelings of guilt and shame over our past—and forgiven—sins.

The devil does not quit simply because we have received salvation.

The only way to remove these feelings of guilt, according to Scripture, is to overcome the devil's accusations through the *"blood of the Lamb"* and by the *"word of* [our] *testimony"* (Revelation 12:11).

There are two aspects brought out in this passage. One is the atonement of Christ. The other is our present testimony of the blood. The first is God's work; the second is our work. We had nothing to do with providing the atonement. That was God's doing. We do, however, have control over our testimony. We can choose to affirm our belief in what Jesus' blood accomplished, or we can deny the power of the blood to work in our lives. Many unknowingly deny the power and work of the blood by choosing to instead remain guilt-stricken over sin. Whether it is a divorce, a crime, or a moral failure, these saints choose to believe their guilt-laden feelings rather than the cross. In short, they can't get over the past. The devil loves it when you act according to your feelings.

"I don't *feel* forgiven," some say. Who cares how you feel? God says you are forgiven; therefore, you must act against your feelings. Instead of accepting forgiveness, some drop out of ministry or simply quit the church itself because they no longer feel worthy to serve. They are led by their feelings of shame and embarrassment.

A testimony is given according to what is seen, heard, or experienced. The saints in Revelation overcame the devil by including the blood in their testimony. You may have heard of the blood of Christ, but in your mind's eye, you should picture His blood cleansing you of your sins. You must testify to this if you wish to be set free from the shame and guilt of your past. Quit confessing that you are "too rotten" to serve the Lord. You need to stop declaring and reliving your sins over and over again. Declare the blood of Jesus, for it has washed you clean!

God Is Greater Than Your Heart

> *This then is…how we set our hearts at rest in his presence whenever our hearts condemn us. For God is greater than our hearts, and he knows everything.* (1 John 3:19–20)

One of the greatest mistakes you can make is to put more stock in the feelings of your heart than in God. God is greater than our hearts. If He says that your sin is taken away, who are you to say it is not?

"But I feel so bad about what I did. I don't feel right serving the church because of what I did."

If this is how you feel, do you see what you are doing? You are taking the condemnation of your heart and putting it above the Word of God. God knows everything, including the fact that you sin, yet He still loves you and wants to

God knows everything, yet He still loves you and wants to restore you to your calling.

restore you to the position of your calling. But He cannot do this if you allow the enemy to keep beating you up for your past. You must realize that the condemnation of your heart is coming directly from the accusations of the devil.

Mental health facilities often house Christians who cannot let go of their pasts. I've met them. They are always talking about some past failure. They have bought the lies of the enemy. They honestly think that God is the one who is angry with them. Little do they know it is the devil, not God, who has been hurling accusations against them.

Bridgett had trouble connecting with other girls her age. Despite being young, she was overweight and was not what others would call pretty. Because of this, the popular girls often made fun of her. To counteract her humiliation, Bridgett found comfort with the boys at her school. She played sports with them and became a rather good athlete. Feeling deficient as a female, she began to idolize different female traits. That idolatry turned sexual, and she began to fantasize about some of the more feminine girls. Being from a Christian home, however, she was frightened by these feelings, and she never acted on them. Instead, she devoted her life to serving people and the church.

Bridgett eventually decided, for her own spiritual health, to join an organization devoted to helping gay and lesbian individuals find healing. During one of the group sessions, the moderator asked how she was doing. She told them how extremely down and dejected she was. She told the group that earlier that morning she had a session with her Christian counselor during which she experienced a real breakthrough. She sprang out of the counselor's office buoyed by the progress she was making. Then, as she was approaching her apartment, a jogger—a beautiful woman with long, flowing hair—ran right in front of her. Bridgett looked at the runner and felt powerfully drawn toward her. As a result, she fell into immediate despair. "God has just done this wonderful work in me, and look at what I am doing, lusting over a woman and desiring her sexually!"

After Bridgett had shared this with the group, the moderator asked her if she had sinned in this situation. She said, "No, but..." She couldn't find the words to complete the sentence; her feelings of guilt and remorse were so great that she knew she had to be guilty of something.

If the devil can flood us with guilt concerning temptation, we are that much closer to succumbing to sin, where the devil has his victory.

The moderator told her what she had probably heard a thousand times: "Temptation is not sin."

Bridgett's response was so similar to many of ours. "Yes, I know, but..."

Intellectually or theologically, we can accept the truth that temptation is not sin, but, in our day-to-day walks, we may feel tremendous guilt for even experiencing such temptation. This is the work of the devil. If he can flood us with guilt concerning temptation, we are that much closer to succumbing to sin, where the devil has his victory.

Like a juror, you have a choice. Who do you believe? Do you believe the feelings of your heart or the Word of God? You must decide who is telling the truth. Is it God, about whom John wrote, *"If we confess our sins, he is faithful and just and will forgive us our sins and purify us from all unrighteousness"* (1 John 1:9)? Or is it your heart, which says, "I have confessed my sin, but I do not feel any differently"?

Naked Christians

The trouble I see with many Christians is that they have initially accepted the cleansing of their sins, but they refuse to put on the clean garments of righteousness. It was not enough for God to remove Joshua's filthy clothes; He also told the angel to put *"rich garments"* on him (Zechariah 3:4). Many Christians see their sins as being forgiven but then walk around naked because they have not put on the robes of righteousness.

"God made him who had no sin to be sin for us, so that in him we might become the righteousness of God" (2 Corinthians 5:21). Most confess that they are unworthy sinners saved by God's grace, but this testimony falls short of the actual work of the cross. The cross made you totally alive; you became a *"new creation"* (verse 17). God does not see the same old you. He does not see an old sinner saved by grace; instead, He sees you as a new creation, living by grace.

You must put on the robe of righteousness and confess who God has remade you to be. "I am the righteousness of God." Go ahead, say it. I know it is hard to say it at first, but you must say it in order to build a realization of the righteousness inside of you. This realization will affect your faith and increase your boldness.

The touching story of the prodigal son reveals this truth. After squandering his father's money on wine, women, and riotous living, he returned home, hoping that his father would take him back as a mere servant. The father did more than that. Not only did the father forgive him, but he also took off his son's filthy clothes and replaced them with festive robes. He put a ring on his son's finger and sandals on his feet. The father not only forgave his son but restored him as a son. He wanted him to "act" like a son—no more begging, no more shame, no more disgrace. It was time to rejoin the family and share in the love and wealth of his father. (See Luke 15:11–32.)

The moment you were born again, you became the righteousness of God. Righteousness gave you certain "rights." With righteousness, you can claim your privileges as a son of God. With boldness, you can tell the devil to take his hands off your property. You can take back his spoils. He has been keeping you bound, sick, and poor. Now that you know who you are in Christ, you can command the

The moment you were born again, you became the righteousness of God.

devil to get his paws off your goods. Jesus said that you are family again, and with His name on your lips, "*You may ask me for anything in my name, and I will do it*" (John 14:14).

Part Two

Demons and Deliverance

Chapter Four

How to Cast out Demons

Jesus was an exorcist.

This presents a great problem that many contemporary churches must resolve—how to acknowledge Jesus' ministry of deliverance without imitating His ministry. This is difficult because Jesus not only cast out demons, but He also gave His disciples this same power and encouraged their successors to do the same. *"And these signs will accompany those who believe: In my name they will drive out demons"* (Mark 16:17). These signs are not for His apostles only, but also for *"those who believe."*

It is one thing for some in the church to have doubts about the existence of miracles today, but how can these people claim that the practice of deliverance is unnecessary when they have no theology to explain demons' disappearance from the earth? It has been my experience that even non-charismatic churches believe that demons exist and that they will be unleashed to a greater extent as we approach the end times. Yet these people choose to completely ignore Jesus' words foretelling that His followers would routinely cast out demons. Even if they choose not to believe in healing or speaking in tongues, how can people ignore the casting out of demons?

Casting out demons is not simply a manifestation of gifts or miracles; it is a necessity. As long as demons are real, the act of casting them out is required of Christians.

There are some who actually argue that the rise of the psychiatric profession has replaced our need to cast out demons. This, however, presents a greater problem for evangelicals, for if psychiatrists have successfully removed demons through medicine and therapy, should we not assume that the kingdom of God has also come through these techniques?

Jesus explained the ultimate conclusion of His ministry of deliverance: "*If I drive out demons by the Spirit of God, then the kingdom of God has come upon you*" (Matthew 12:28).

Casting out demons is not simply a manifestation of gifts or miracles; it is a necessity.

None of the Old Testament prophets performed exorcisms. They carried out miracles of nature but never cast out demons. This act was reserved as proof that the Messiah had arrived, for no sinner had the authority to give orders to these spiritual beings. Jesus trumped the miracles of the Old Testament by driving out demons. When we exercise this power and authority in His name, we, too, demonstrate that we belong to the kingdom of God.

Since I have appeared on national television, I am often asked about the ministry of deliverance. It is my sincere desire to provide practical and biblically based teaching in this area. The best way to learn about casting out demons is by studying Jesus' ministry. Let's go back two thousand years and examine the first example of deliverance.

Jesus' First Encounter

When the Sabbath came, Jesus went into the synagogue and began to teach. The people were amazed at his teaching, because he taught them as one who had authority, not as the teachers of the law. Just then a man in their synagogue who was possessed by an evil spirit cried out, "What do you want with us, Jesus of Nazareth? Have you come to destroy us? I know who you are—the Holy One of God!" "Be quiet!" said Jesus sternly. "Come out of him!" The evil spirit shook the man violently and came out of him with a shriek. The people were all so amazed that they asked each other, "What is this? A new teaching—and with authority! He even gives orders to evil spirits and they obey him." (Mark 1:21–27)

Many modern psychologists try to explain these Scriptures by saying that the people in Jesus' day did not know anything about mental disorders, so they created the concept of demons to explain people's mental illnesses. It was not, however, just the people in those days who believed in demon possession—Jesus also acknowledged their reality. If demons were not real, then Jesus, the Son of God, was deceived and wrong and therefore could not have been the sinless Savior of the world.

Some so-called theologians have espoused the theory that when Jesus took on our humanity, He also took on the ignorance and superstition of mankind, including superstitions about demons. This theory is hard to swallow. It is one thing to say that Jesus became one with our humanity, but it is another thing to say that He partook of our errors and ignorance. Scripture says, *"Christ* [is]...*the wisdom of God"* (1 Corinthians 1:24); therefore, He had no part in human ignorance or superstition.

In truth, it is the doubters of the demonic who are ignorant about evil spirits. They seem to reason that if something can't be seen, it must not exist. The Bible never claims that spirits can be seen through their manifestations in people's lives.

At the same time, I understand the concern of the psychiatric field when it comes to deliverance. They are worried that people may be hurt by an exorcism more than they are helped. In this, I would agree, so I will offer my counsel and guidance to those who want to be used in the ministry of deliverance.

The Ministry of Deliverance

Spiritual deliverance must be carried out in agreement with Scripture. The harm that has been caused by so-called experts or ministers of deliverance is a result of delving into extra-biblical, or worse, unbiblical practices.

A nationally syndicated talk show once asked me to share my view on the tragic death of Ronald Marquez, a man who tried to cast demons out of his granddaughter in 2007. Police officers were called to the home because relatives were concerned about how Marquez was attempting to exorcise the demons from the three-year-old. When they arrived, the officers heard screaming coming from the bedroom. They had trouble getting into the room, however, because Marquez had pushed a bed against the door to keep out the doubters. Once the officers had pushed open the door, they discovered Marquez strangling his granddaughter as his daughter, naked and bloody, chanted religious prayers. Marquez died from the effects of a taser the police used to force him to release his grip on his granddaughter.

Spiritual deliverance must be carried out in agreement with Scripture.

Clearly, this was an ignorant and misguided attempt to cast out demons. I told the interviewer that it appeared that Marquez and his daughter may have been the ones who needed deliverance. The only example of demon possession and nudity in the Bible is the madman of Gadarenes, and he was the one with the demons. (See Mark 5:1–19.)

Because of instances such as the Marquez case, there is a need for biblically based teaching on how to cast out demons. Scripture gives us several important facts about Jesus' ministry of exorcism. If we follow His example, we will see positive results.

1. Jesus focused on teaching and preaching, not deliverance, but, when the need arose, He drove out demons.

In the story of this first deliverance, the reason Jesus came into the synagogue was to *teach*. The Bible says that the people *"were amazed at his teaching"* (Mark 1:22). Today, I'm dismayed by the lack of teaching about deliverance among ministers and pastors.

There are some who believe they should specialize in deliverance. I don't agree. Exorcism should never be a specialty. Every minister should teach the Word of God to people, and, when the need arises, drive out demons. There is no need to go to "Sister Deliverance" whenever someone needs to be set free from demons. These specialists seem to have a sign that reads: "Bring your paper sack with you and prepare to vomit your demons." Unfortunately, these people aren't able to remain demon-free because of a lack of the Word. Understand, I have seen people vomit after they have been delivered, but I don't look for it.

Some ask, "Why does it seem that people cough or vomit whenever demons come out?" I explain that there is scriptural precedent for physical manifestations. The Bible says, *"The evil spirit shook the man violently and came out of him with a shriek"* (Mark 1:26). It is normal for there to be physical manifestations when spirits come out, especially physical manifestations through the mouth. This is exactly what happened when Philip drove out spirits. *"With shrieks, evil spirits came out of many"* (Acts 8:7). It seems that the usual exit for evil spirits is through the mouth. After all, it is usually our big mouths that opened the door for them to enter in the first place. It only stands to reason that the mouth would be the exit, too. Coughing and vomiting are also manifestations of the mouth.

In my youth, I worked at a local restaurant, and one of my fellow employees once confided in me. "Tom," she said, "I know that you're going to think I'm crazy, but I feel that I have a demon inside of me. Nearly every night when I go to bed, this spirit begins to scare me." This girl was not a charismatic. She was not even a Christian at the time. She simply believed that evil spirits were real.

Exorcism should never be a specialty. Every minister should teach the Word of God to people, and, when the need arises, drive out demons.

I told her I believed her, and that I would try to help. We ended the conversation and continued working. Later, after we closed the restaurant and started cleaning up, the Lord spoke to me, saying, "Tom, if you will speak to the spirit now, the demon will go."

I walked up to this girl as she was vacuuming the carpet. I said to her, "The Lord spoke to me and told me to tell the spirit to go, and it will."

She turned off the vacuum cleaner and said, "Okay. Tell it to go."

I pointed my finger at her—she was about ten feet away—and said to the spirit, "In the name of Jesus, I tell you, evil spirit, to come out of her!"

The moment I said that, she gasped, "Ugh!" Startled, she exclaimed, "Something came out of my mouth. What was that?"

"That was the demon. It's gone!"

Let me repeat. This girl knew *nothing* of the charismatic movement. She had never seen people delivered from evil spirits. She had no past experience that would have caused her to think that the demon should come out of her mouth. But it did. This incident is similar to biblical examples of shrieking.

In most of the deliverances I've been involved in, the demons came out of people with shrieks. This includes screaming, yelling, growling, snarling, and similar vocal noises. On the other hand, I don't force or encourage people to do anything. I simply tell them to be set free.

2. Jesus drove out demons regularly.

> *That evening after sunset the people brought to Jesus all the sick and demon-possessed. The whole town gathered at the door, and Jesus healed many who had various diseases. He also drove out many demons, but he would not let the demons speak because they knew who he was.* (Mark 1:32–34)

Jesus "*drove out many demons.*" Some people get the false impression that there are not that many demons, and what few there are remain huddled in Third World countries, away from enlightened and sophisticated society. A famous Christian psychiatrist wrote,

I can honestly say that I have never yet seen a single case of demon possession...I believe that there probably are some demon possessed persons in various parts of the world.

I have had hundreds of patients who came to see me because they thought they were demon possessed. Scores of them heard "demon voices" telling them evil things to do. It was at first surprising to me that all of these had dopamine deficiencies in their brains, which were readily correctable with Thorazine or any other major tranquilizer.[1]

Why do some demons stop manifesting themselves when the patients take tranquilizers? I have talked with many of these people on medication, and some have told me the voices did not stop. They may not have been as loud, but the voices continued. The reason the voices soften is because people are sedated. The patient's personality is restrained. It is like the people of Gadara who bound the demoniac with chains so that he would not hurt himself and others. The chains did not free the man; they only restrained the demons from fully taking over. Medication may provide temporary relief from the voices of demons, but the permanent answer to

Medication may provide temporary relief from demons, but the permanent answer to their eviction is found in complete deliverance by God.

---

1 Danny Korem and Paul Meier, *The Fakers*, as quoted in Josh McDowell and Don Stewart, *Handbook of Today's Religions*, 178.

their eviction is only found in complete deliverance by the power of God.

In some cases, I believe the problem is completely physiological. I've found that if the voices stop completely and the person "gets better," then I doubt the problem was demons in the first place. Demons will not be removed by taking medication. I often counsel such people to continue taking the medication if it is working and to quit looking for demons in their lives.

3. Jesus did not drive out demons from everyone.

In the case of the demoniac in the synagogue, Jesus only drove demons out of the one man. No one else was delivered. He did not hand out bags to everyone and say, "All right, people, get ready to be delivered."

It seems that the body of Christ can't find the middle ground on this topic. They fall into a ditch on one side or the other. Some claim that it is impossible for Christians to be possessed; others declare that everyone has demons. In my experience, neither position is right.

Demons do inhabit many, but not most people.

Demons do inhabit many, but not most people. For example, there is no mention about any of the apostles, except perhaps Judas, ever having demons. They were humans who made mistakes and did dumb things, but never once did demons possess them. The closest thing to demon possession in their lives was when Christ rebuked Peter. Jesus said to him, *"Get behind me, Satan!"* (Matthew 16:23). Jesus spoke directly to Satan, who used Peter, but did not drive out demons from him.

4. Jesus did not chat with demons.

In Mark 5, Jesus said to the demon, *"Come out of this man, you evil spirit!"* (verse 8). The usual way of speaking to demons is to give them a simple order. In this case, Jesus went on by asking the demon, *"What is your name?"* (verse 9). This is sometimes helpful, especially when the demon is putting up a fierce fight.

Occasionally, I also ask the demon to give me its name so that I can understand what it is doing in the victim. The names usually relate to their activities, such as "Lust," "Hate," "Murder," etc. Rarely will I hear the demons use the vocal cords of their hosts to tell me their names; in most cases, I hear their names in the spirit.

Often, when I speak the specific names of the demon or demons, the person being prayed for will react as though he is surprised that I know the problem. At this point, the person usually receives his or her deliverance within minutes.

I do not find any cases in the Bible where the Lord held conversations with demons, so I do not think it is wise to engage them in dialogue. In most cases, Jesus ordered them to remain silent. Let me share with you an experience that illustrates the futility of holding conversations with demons.

My Personal Experience

Once, someone came pounding on my door. As I opened it, one of my church members barged through, yelling, "Tom, you have to come with me quickly! There's a man who is demon possessed. We need your help to drive them out!" I went with him.

When I arrived, there were about four men who were trying to exorcise the demons from this man. Everyone was shouting different things: "What's your name?" "Tell us about the realm of the spirit." "Where did you come from?" "Recount to us the role of demons in Mexico." Everyone seemed more interested in talking with the demons than casting them out. Whenever they would try to hold the man down, the demoniac simply threw them across the room. One of them turned to me and said, "Tom, these demons don't want to leave. We've been at it for several hours. Why don't you give it a try? Maybe you can cast them out."

I walked over to this man, reached out my right hand, and touched his shoulder. Looking him in the eyes, I said, "I'm not talking to the demons, I'm talking to you, sir. Please come over here to the couch and sit down with me." He did.

I asked him, "How long have you been like this?"

"For many years, I have heard these demons talk to me and speak through me. I want to be free, but I can't."

"Yes, you can!" I assured him. "And I believe that you will be set free today."

"Can you drive the demons out of me?"

"I can, with God's power."

He grinned, "I think you can."

"I know I can." I laid my hands on the man and said calmly, yet sternly, "In the name of Jesus, I command all the evil spirits to come out of him." I named several that I believed were in him. As soon as I said that, the man looked up at me with a wide smile. "They're gone!" he exclaimed. The other men also sensed that the spirits had left him.

That night, the leader of this group came to me privately and asked, "Tom, what were we doing wrong? Why couldn't we drive out the spirits?"

I explained to him, "You should not hold conversations with demons. By doing so, you prolong the deliverance. Simply take authority over the spirits and cast them out!" He accepted what I said.

5. Jesus drove out demons with His word.

When Jesus drove out the demon from the man in the synagogue, the people were astonished. They said, "He even gives orders to evil spirits and they obey him" (Mark 1:27). They weren't used to demons being ordered about with mere words, but that is exactly how Jesus delivered people. Another Scripture says, "When evening came,

The only method you need is your mouth. Your words can drive out demons.

many who were demon-possessed were brought to him, and he [Jesus] drove out the spirits with a word and healed all the sick" (Matthew 8:16).

Jesus expelled demons simply by His word; He used nothing else. I'm often surprised when I see Christians depending on various exotic methods for casting out demons. The only method you need is your mouth. Your words can drive out demons.

Still, there are those who try to perform exorcisms like they've seen it done in movies—with holy water, a crucifix, candles, incense, prayer beads, or anything else they think might be effective in driving out demons. There is one crucial thing they lack: faith.

Perverting Exorcism

The Bible records one instance when the disciples failed to drive out a demon from a boy. When Jesus arrived and saw the boy was still possessed, He rebuked the disciples and said, *"O unbelieving and perverse generation"* (Matthew 17:17). Notice that Jesus not only called them unbelieving, but He also called them *"perverse."* The word *perverse* means "something inherently good that has been twisted into something bad." Christ expected His disciples to use His name to drive out demons. Evidently, the disciples must have resorted to other means, perhaps to some of the more elaborate methods of Jewish exorcism.

Jesus told us to depend only on His name. Christians are not to depend on anything else. His name has the authority to make demons bow. With the power of the Holy Spirit and your knowledge of the Word of God, you have everything you will ever need to drive out demons successfully.

Chapter Five

Can Christians Have Demons?

This is the number one question I hear people ask.

In answering, I like to point out that Jesus' first successful attempt to drive out a demon was from a man in a synagogue, not in some pagan "voodoo" ceremony. This man was in an orthodox, Jewish place of worship.

In those days, it was the practice to exclude from attending synagogue all who were not "preapproved" by the Pharisees. When Jesus was criticized for spending time with lepers, tax collectors, and prostitutes, it was because such people were deemed "unclean" and would not have been allowed in the house of God. Even a man who became a believer in God could not enter the synagogue unless he went through a full Jewish conversion, including circumcision. Thus, if Jesus' first deliverance took place within a synagogue, it must have been for an orthodox, Jewish believer.

Some might point out that this person may have been Jewish, but he was not a Christian. They hold to the belief that an authentically born-again Christian who is owned by God cannot be possessed by a demon, because *possess* implies ownership, and only God owns the believer.

What Is Demon Possession?

Let's start by defining the term *demon possession.* As many scholars have pointed out, the word *possession* has no equivalent in the original Greek language. It was added by early translators and it has consequently taken on multiple meanings and understandings. People rarely use any other word but *possession* in describing someone beset by demons. The Greek word used actually means "demonize." *Strong's Concordance* suggests another possible meaning: "to vex." *Vex* means "to irritate, annoy, or provoke; to torment, trouble, or worry." Such vexation may simply be a demon on the "outside" tempting or harassing the believer, similar to Paul's thorn in the flesh. Paul called this *"a messenger of Satan, to torment me"* (2 Corinthians 12:7). The demon was not inside Paul, but it seemed to be on the outside, trying to stir up trouble for him. In this case, the *"messenger of Satan"* was stirring up persecution against Paul. Most will not dispute the possibility that demons may afflict believers from the outside; they have difficulty, however, believing that demons could reside inside believers.

> *It is in the arena of thoughts that demons primarily work.*

Again, we need to define what is meant by *inside.* There are a lot of things inside me: my organs, for sure, but also my thoughts and emotions. It is in the arena of thoughts that demons primarily work. This is why most of the cases of demonization in the Bible are often described as some sort of insanity, mental illness, or emotional condition. Why is it difficult to accept the fact that demons may be infecting the thought life of an individual?

Of course, the most important thing inside me is my spirit. Let me make it clear that I do not believe a demon can inhabit the spirit of a born-again Christian. My spirit is the part of me that has been born again. My body was not reborn, nor was my mind. The Bible says, *"If anyone is in Christ, he is a new creation"* (2 Corinthians 5:17). What part of me has become a new creation? Certainly not my body. I still have the same old body that I had when I was first saved, although it's getting older and weaker. My mind, though it has seen changes, it not a "new creation." Paul was encouraging believers to do something about both their bodies and minds:

> *Therefore, I urge you, brothers, in view of God's mercy, to offer your bodies as living sacrifices, holy and pleasing to God—this is your spiritual act of worship. Do not conform any longer to the pattern of this world, but be transformed by the renewing of your mind.* (Romans 12:1–2)

According to Paul, a believer, after conversion, still has the responsibility to work with his body and mind. What happens when the believer refuses to offer his body as a living sacrifice or to renew his mind? Could this possibly open the door for demons to take advantage, especially if he has indulged in the lust of the flesh or entertained wrong thoughts? In such cases, I think it is reasonable to assume that demons could take advantage of a believer.

While I would agree that a demon cannot *possess* a believer in the sense of "ownership," this does not mean that a demon cannot *vex* a believer. Most theologians would agree with this, as long as the vexation occurs from outside of the believer. Deliverance is not necessary, however, if a demon is on the *outside*. All that is needed in such a case is for the believer to simply resist the demon and it will leave. But when a demon is *inside* of the believer, he will need help from others to gain the victory. Such help is called *deliverance*.

> *While I would agree that a demon cannot possess a believer in the sense of "ownership," this does not mean that a demon cannot vex a believer.*

The main difference that distinguishes inner demons from outer ones is in the area of self-control. Does the believer still have control to remove the demon? If he does, the demon is on the outside. When a demon is on the inside, that person loses part of his control. This can occur through drugs, alcohol, pornography, lust, gluttony, anger, or other life-controlling addictions. At this point, it is not very far down the road to things like physical and sexual abuse, rape, incest, homosexuality, and a host of other dangerous behaviors. Someone caught in this cycle—one in which he feels hopeless to change—will often require deliverance. (We will further discuss the issue of self-control in chapter 8.)

Another sign that demons are working from within is if the person has the feeling that another personality is working within him to make him do things he would not normally do. Some have told me of the despicable acts they have done under demonic control. Many say they felt as though they were bystanders watching their bodies do these things. It was as if someone other than themselves was doing the act.

Angela

Angela was a new mother who appeared normal until she felt a strange personality enter into her. She began to exhibit strange behavior. She started to talk as though another person were using her vocal cords. Her husband did not know exactly what to do, but he reported his wife's strange behavior to her mother. He wondered if it might have been postpartum depression. Even so, why the voices? Having heard me on radio, the mother had written down our number in case she ever needed prayer. She needed it now!

I remember taking the call. It was late at night and I could hear screaming in the background. I tried to calm the mother, but she kept insisting that her daughter was possessed! What I heard seemed to confirm the woman's assessment. I jotted down the address and went to their home, accompanied by my wife.

When I arrived, I saw the oppressed woman crouched on the couch, growling and looking at me with intense eyes. I approached the woman and turned to question her husband, who was confused and didn't understand what was happening. He was a man with little faith or knowledge of God's Word.

I then spoke clearly to the evil spirit and told it to leave. To her husband's amazement, the spirit left Angela and she immediately returned to her right mind. She didn't remember anything that had happened, asking who I was and why I was in their home. The entire incident was a complete blank for her. She mentioned how she had been feeling depressed after having her baby, and she had a vague recollection of some entity entering her. While postpartum depression is a real medical condition, this woman clearly had more than just the "new mother blues." She needed deliverance.

Why Do Christians Seem to Be the Ones Delivered?

Because many reject the notion that Christians can be inhabited by demons, they also conclude that the practice of deliverance cannot be of God. Many people will ask for one biblical example of a full-fledged Christian who needed deliverance after Pentecost. Since there is no record of such a person in the book of Acts, they conclude that Christians cannot have demons.

The book of Acts, however, was not intended to be an instruction book on deliverance, but simply a historical overview of the spread of Christianity. It tells of how the Gentiles were incorporated into the church without the requirement of becoming fully Jewish. It details the persecution of the early church and of the creation of new churches. Any instance of Christians in need of deliverance is thus beyond the scope of the book. Just because deliverance is not dealt with, however, does not mean that it did not exist. Thankfully, we do have a biblical account of demonic deliverance, and, using this account, we can use simple logic to come up with some answers to these questions.

Philip's Ministry of Deliverance

Philip went down to a city in Samaria and proclaimed the Christ there. When the crowds heard Philip and saw the miraculous signs he did, they all paid close attention to what he said. With shrieks, evil spirits came out of many, and many paralytics and cripples were healed. So there was great joy in that city. (Acts 8:5–8)

The people in Samaria needed deliverance. Not just a few; rather, there were many who needed it. When Philip arrived, he drove out many demons from those people and brought to them the saving work of Christ. Again, critics will maintain that Philip was driving demons out of sinners, and I will agree. However, he also gave us an important precedent for evangelism. While the contemporary church normally bypasses deliverance and goes straight to conversion and baptism, Philip recognized the need to deliver sinners from demons before bringing them into a full conversion.

Christians may need deliverance if demons were not driven out before their conversion.

This passage also explores another very real possibility: Christians may need deliverance if demons were not driven out before their conversion. Some might suggest that once sinners are saved, any demons must automatically leave. If that were the case, then why did Philip bother to cast out demons at all if converting them would have done the trick? It would seem that Philip was wasting his time by driving out the demons when he could have just shared the gospel with the people.

I believe that the modern day evangelical movement has neglected exercising this important ministry. Instead of following Philip's example, they bypass the sinners' need for deliverance and quickly bring them into baptism and all the other ordinances. We have a right, however, to question this pattern of evangelism: preach the gospel, lead the sinners in a prayer, baptize them, and usher them into membership in the church. What if demons were active in their lives? Do we ignore that possibility?

> *Without dealing with their demons, Christians often fail to live up to the potential of what it means to be a follower of Christ.*

It troubles me that we see so many believers who are in need of deliverance. I suspect the real culprit is the failure of gospel ministers to deliver them of demons before they are converted. Without this step, we are now stuck after the fact, trying to bring deliverance to them. Those of us within the deliverance movement then get reprimanded by heresy hunters for driving demons out of Christians who should have received deliverance by the ministers who brought them to Christ. It is not our fault, or the fault of the converts, that the modern pattern of evangelicalism strays from the biblical pattern of deliverance. Thus, it does not surprise me that so many Christians need deliverance.

I would estimate that more than half of the deliverances I have performed were on Christians who had demons influencing their lives prior to salvation. In most cases, I find that their problems started even before their born-again experiences. It is only after I minister to them that they experience freedom from the demons of their pasts.

When critics insist on the impossibility of Christians having demons, they must also be honest about the failure of the church to deal thoroughly with demonic activity in the lives of believers. Without dealing with their demons, Christians often fail to live up to the potential of what it means to be a follower of Christ. Deliverance may be their only solution. I find it useless to argue against their need for deliverance on the sole grounds that their conversion experiences have automatically removed all the demons from their lives.

Jim

Jim was a wonderful pastor; he and his wife absolutely loved the Lord. I was surprised, however, to hear how they came to Christ. They had been practicing New Age beliefs before they were saved. In fact, they were not merely dabblers in such things but leaders in the movement. After seeing how entrenched their lives were in the lie, they saw the truth and found Christ.

The minister who led them to Christ, however, did not practice deliverance, so while they loved the Lord, there were still demons influencing their lives. These demons were working to destroy their marriage and confuse them in their walk with God.

It wasn't until they attended a gathering of Full Gospel Business Men that they saw the truth about demons in their lives. There they heard the story of a man's deliverance, and they rightly perceived that they, too, needed deliverance. They came forward, and, the moment they were prayed for, all the voices of the demons began to speak through this couple. Within minutes, they were completely free.

After being delivered, they found it much easier to grow in the Lord. They found a new hunger for the Word of God that had not been there before. Today, they are serving the Lord full-time, sharing the gospel in their little town.

The first issue, therefore, is not whether or not demons can enter a Christian, but whether they may remain in a Christian if they were not expelled when the individual was saved. From Philip's example in Acts, we have clearly seen the danger in bringing people to the Lord without first driving out any demonic activity; otherwise, those demons will come directly into the church.

Chapter Six

Open Doors for Demons

As stated in the previous chapter, there is no indication in Scripture that demons *automatically* leave a person when he is saved. This idea of "automatic deliverance" is not only unbiblical, it is also dangerous, and it may lead to two terrible consequences: first, it will force people to suppress their root problem; second, they will develop a false sense of security.

Imagine that you are taught that believers cannot have demons, and yet you have all the characteristics of demonization. You would be forced to deny or ignore all the feelings within. This only leads to other spiritual problems. Instead of spending the necessary time trying to grow as a Christian, you would find yourself exerting the majority of your spiritual energy trying to suppress the demons. You would work overtime on trying to put up a good front for the church, thinking that your pastor and fellow congregants don't want to face the reality of their false doctrine that Christians cannot have demons.

The movie *Unbreakable*, starring Bruce Willis, typifies the problem that stems from believing that you are unconditionally immune from demons. Willis's character,

David Dunn, discovers a numbing truth: no harm can come to him, no matter what he does. He lives his life constantly facing extreme dangers because he feels invincible. Unfortunately, his life lacks the passion that comes with the risk of loss. There is no excitement to living if you cannot fail. It's like watching a taped game of your favorite sports team—it's not as exciting if you already know the outcome before you watch the game. Even if your team won, you would not feel much excitement in watching the game. The thrill comes from the possibility of losing.

Demons can attack you, and if you believe the lie that they can't, you will take risks with your own soul because you think you are invincible.

Worse things, however, can occur from being mistakenly told that you are automatically immune from demons. Your risky behavior will only open you up to additional demonization. In truth, demons can attack you, and if you believe the lie that they can't, you will take risks with your own soul because you think you are invincible. Instead of being vigilant and protecting yourself from the strategies of the devil, you will flippantly ignore the danger and take your enemy for granted, allowing the demons to take advantage of your overly confident behavior.

Temple of the Holy Spirit

Another argument is that demons can't enter Christians because they are the temples of the Holy Spirit. That is true—if we keep our bodies pure. Surely no demon will enter our undefiled bodies. The trouble comes when believers yield to fleshly sins. As they do, they open themselves to demonic activity.

Practicing a Sinful Lifestyle

It's interesting to note that the passage that says Christians are the temples of the Holy Spirit was written to warn Christians from committing sexual sins. Paul said, *"Flee from sexual immorality....Do you not know that your body is a temple of the Holy Spirit?...Therefore honor God with your body"* (1 Corinthians 6:18–20).

This passage in no way implies that demons cannot inhabit the believer's body. On the contrary, this passage encourages believers to keep their bodies pure for the Holy Spirit so that they will not become habitations for demons. In the same letter, the apostle Paul said,

> *I do not want you to be participants with demons. You cannot drink the cup of the Lord and the cup of demons too; you cannot have a part in both the Lord's table and the table of demons. Are we trying to arouse the Lord's jealousy? Are we stronger than he?* (1 Corinthians 10:20–22)

This passage would be meaningless if Christians were automatically immune from demons. Why warn believers about being *"participants with demons"* if they are not capable of being participants with them? Paul said you cannot take part in both tables. He wasn't saying it is not *possible;* he was saying it is not *right* to do so. When a Christian practices what is not right, he creates an opportunity for demons to work in

Since demons are sinful, they prefer to work with those who also practice sin as a lifestyle.

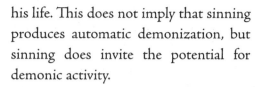

his life. This does not imply that sinning produces automatic demonization, but sinning does invite the potential for demonic activity.

There is a finite number of demons in the world. They cannot, therefore, inhabit every person on the earth. Instead, they find it easier to manifest their personalities through those who are more inclined to allow sin into their lives. Since demons are sinful, they prefer to work with those who also practice sin as a lifestyle. This is true for sinners as well as believers.

Worse Off than an Unbeliever

> *If they have escaped the corruption of the world by knowing our Lord and Savior Jesus Christ and are again entangled in it and overcome, they are worse off at the end than they were at the beginning.*

(2 Peter 2:20)

This passage is a sobering reminder for Christians who return to the ways of the world. The apostle Peter said that such people are worse off in the end than they were at the beginning. He went on to say,

> *It would have been better for them not to have known the way of righteousness, than to have known it and then to turn their backs on the sacred command that was passed on to them.* (verse 21)

What a horrible prospect. You know it's bad when the Bible says it would have been better if you had not been saved in the first place.

The reasons are simple. First, Christians are more accountable to God because they know the truth, as opposed to those who have yet to acknowledge the truth. Second, believers are prime targets for demons. If demons can bring their influence on believers, it will discredit the name of Christ. What better way to harm the reputation and effectiveness of the church than for Satan to send demons to inhabit believers?

Demons love it when believers return to sinful patterns for it gives them an opportunity to damage people and to dishonor the gospel.

Demons love it when believers return to their sinful patterns, for it gives them an opportunity to further damage people as well as a chance to dishonor the gospel. It's disheartening to hear

stories of Christians who have gone mad—killing their spouses, molesting children, delving into homosexuality, or committing other immoral and illegal activities.

Christine

After becoming a Christian at an early age, Christine served in the church with her musical talents, helped the homeless, gave regularly to missionaries, and interceded on behalf of the lost. She devoted no less than two and half hours a day to biblical studies.

Everything seemed to be going well until she met a man—a foreign minister—whom she thought felt the same way that she did about the Lord. Although their relationship was primarily long-distance, the man convinced Christine to marry him. On their honeymoon, she woke up to the realization that her new husband was an abuser who insisted on displaying sadistic behavior from day one. Although Christine had difficulty living this way, she tried to please him, even doing things that went against her conscience. Her compromise was not enough for her husband, however. Soon, he was seeing other women, not caring if Christine knew about it. Eventually, he left her and admitted that the only reason he had married her was to become an American citizen. Christine was devastated! She felt betrayed, not only by this man, but by God. How could God have allowed this man to take advantage of her?

In her resentment, she began to associate with anti-Christian people, including a political activist group opposed to the spread of Christianity. She met a witch in the group who befriended her. She allowed the witch to put a spell on her, supposedly to bring a blessing. That "blessing" only gave Christine a deep desire to experiment sexually, and she became involved with various men and even participated in sexual orgies.

Christine became so disgusted with her new lifestyle that she began to cut herself with a knife. Eventually, she developed thoughts of suicide. On her computer, Christine typed the word *suicide* in search engines and found many different Web sites. Then, she typed "Will suicide send me to hell?" That led her to a Web site that put the fear of God back in her, yet it also gave her hope. The minister wrote about God and His unconditional love, and, slowly, Christine began to desire a relationship with God again.

At first, the sexual demons wouldn't let her go. Christine wondered how she could serve God without the physical pleasures she had experienced with the demons. With the help of a minister, however, Christine was able to get free, and she is now serving the Lord with great enthusiasm.

Do not think for a moment that Christians like Christine are immune to demonic activity. I have often dealt with believers who have experienced a glorious deliverance, while the rest of Christendom ignored the demons in them because it went against their "automatic immunity" theology.

Embracing False Teaching

The Spirit clearly says that in later times some will abandon the faith and follow deceiving spirits and things taught by demons. (1 Timothy 4:1)

As bad as it is to watch people follow deceiving spirits and things taught by demons, it is worse to watch a believer who once embraced the truth abandon his faith and follow the doctrine of demons.

There is no way for one to abandon the faith if he was not, at one time, part of the faith. According to the passage, the reason people desert the faith is because they hold to *"things taught by demons."* Doesn't it seem likely that such a person might be vexed by demons, even having demons inhabit his body or mind? After all, if he embraces the doctrine of demons, isn't it likely he has demons within him?

There are Christians today who have been deceived by the teachings of demons, which can lead them into a kind of demonic bondage. Praise God that there is still hope for them to be set free from deception. Paul's church in Galatia was one that was deceived by false teaching. Paul never considered them as having abandoned the faith but simply as having fallen away from the truth: "*You have fallen away from grace*" (Galatians 5:4).

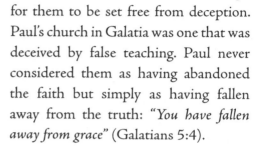

There are Christians today who have been deceived by the teachings of demons, which can lead into a kind of demonic bondage.

There is a real distinction between abandoning one's faith and falling away from it. To abandon something is to leave it on purpose. To fall away implies being tricked. The outcome is similar—both live their lives being deceived by spirits and things taught by demons. There is hope, however, for those who have fallen.

Concerning the Galatian church, the apostle Paul wrote, "*Evidently some people are throwing you into confusion and are trying to pervert the gospel of Christ*" (Galatians 1:7). *Confusion* describes the sincere believer who is being deceived.

> *For if someone comes to you and preaches a Jesus other than the Jesus we preached, or if you receive a different spirit from the one you received, or a different gospel from the one you accepted, you put up with it easily enough.* (2 Corinthians 11:4)

When a person hears a *"different gospel,"* he will receive a *"different spirit"* from the one he should receive. The Spirit we receive by accepting the true gospel is the Holy Spirit. Paul, however, described the church as receiving a different spirit—clearly a reference to evil spirits and things taught by demons.

If one embraces false teaching, it is possible to receive an evil spirit.

Paul was writing to a Corinthian church that had definitely received the Holy Spirit. He had already commended them as a church that did *"not lack any spiritual gift"* (1 Corinthians 1:7). Even though the church had evidences of the Holy Spirit, Paul later warned them about embracing a different Jesus, which would result in them receiving a different spirit from the one they first accepted. If one embraces false teaching, therefore, it is possible to receive an evil spirit after having received the Holy Spirit.

Karen

At the age of ten, Karen experienced an epiphany with the Lord after watching the movie *The Ten Commandments.* Believing in miracles, she said a prayer for a little kitten that she had accidentally poisoned. As the cat foamed at the mouth, Karen knelt beside her pet and prayed for a half hour that God would raise the kitten from the dead. Seeing no results, she finally got up, dried her tears, and headed out the door. When she turned back, the kitten was alive and standing on all fours. From that moment, Karen knew God was real.

As a junior in high school, Karen made friends with a neighborhood girl who was a Mormon. One week, she attended her friend's church, where she was impressed by the Mormons' emphasis on marriage and family. Since her own family was in shambles, Karen found this emphasis very appealing. Eventually, she joined the Mormon church, where she met a friendly man named Bob, who seemed to be the epitome of integrity.

They were later married and spent their honeymoon at the Beehive House, a home that Brigham Young once inhabited while president of the church. A woman giving the tour of the house told them that in the Celestial Kingdom, men will have more than one wife. This revelation did not settle well with Karen. She went home and cried because she couldn't stand the thought that in the life to come, Bob would be married to many wives. Karen decided to try her best to suppress such thoughts as she and Bob settled into married life, had four children, and continued to serve the church faithfully for the next twenty years.

One day, Bob came home and told Karen that he had doubts about the Mormon church. She couldn't believe her ears! She begged him to talk with the elders and even the bishop. He agreed, and he met with the bishop, to whom he explained all he had discovered about the origin of the church, and how it was all a lie.

Even though the couple has now left the Mormon church and joined a Christian church, Karen still feels as though Mormonism has a hold on her. Though she can't explain it, this grip has caused her to contemplate suicide.

She describes her relationship with the Lord as half full. She is optimistic about the future, but, in my opinion, she needs complete deliverance.

Unfortunately, there are many people like Karen who have come out of the darkness but have yet to experience the total deliverance they need. They have picked up bad spirits from false teachings. To ignore these deceiving spirits is to do an injustice to those who are trying to escape such heretical doctrine.

Some of the most common types of false teachings today are from eastern religions, often cloaked in New Age concepts. Hinduism seems especially prone to attract demons, as do witchcraft, psychics, and other forms of the occult, such as Scientology. Pseudo-Christian groups may talk about Jesus, but they are actually referring another Jesus. The real Jesus is the Son of God, the second Person of the Trinity. He is not the "spirit brother" of Satan, or Michael the archangel, as Mormons and Jehovah's Witnesses argue.

Contemporary churches seem alarmingly susceptible to false teaching, in part because there is so little sound, biblical preaching.

The contemporary church seems alarmingly susceptible to false teaching, in part because there is so little sound, biblical preaching on the foundations of Christianity. Instead, many churches feel the need to emphasize non-controversial, easy-to-swallow, feel-good messages in order to attract and maintain large crowds.

The apostle Paul warned us about the days in which we live, saying,

> *For the time will come when men will not put up with sound doctrine. Instead, to suit their own desires, they will gather around them a great number of teachers to say what their itching ears want to hear. They will turn their ears away from the truth and turn aside to myths.*

(2 Timothy 4:3–4)

Today, we have an abundance of religious and spiritual teachers who, like good marketing agents, simply tell their audiences what they want to hear. There is little interest in deep theological teaching, so they give the people what they *want*, not what they *need*. This environment opens the door to false teachers who are eager to fill the vacuum with erroneous teachings about God and salvation. False teaching opens wide the door to the realm of the demonic.

Chapter Seven

Two Extreme Views
Concerning Deliverance

One of the hardest things for people to do, especially when it comes to issues of spiritual deliverance, is to maintain balance—to walk the narrow path without falling into the ditch on either side.

Hyperdeliverance and Nondeliverance

For some who discover the ministry of deliverance, it quickly becomes a cure-all for anything and everything. Some will make deliverance the "only" truth in the Bible. I call this viewpoint *hyperdeliverance*. Deliverance is biblical; it is good; it is needed. It is possible, however, to go overboard by trying to apply it when it is not necessary, which can do more harm than good.

On the other hand, some people fall into the pit where deliverance is disregarded altogether. These people talk about the devil but never confront him directly. They do not cast out demons, even though Scripture commands them to do so. They develop a philosophical, theological position to justify their stance. Their defense, however, often lacks real theology and is mostly philosophical. They have departed from the Bible and are depending on their logic and tradition. I call this viewpoint *nondeliverance.*

The hyperdeliverance group sees nearly all problems as stemming from Satan and few, if any, as stemming from natural causes. The nondeliverance camp views nearly all problems as either naturally occurring or from God's own sovereign hand. They speak much of God's sovereignty but mention very little about spiritual warfare or the possibility that Satan could be behind certain problems in their lives.

The hyperdeliverance crowd views nearly all sickness as having demonic origins, giving little thought to their diets, amount of exercise, or lifestyles. Medicine is often shunned as a repudiation of the gospel's power. On the other hand, the nondeliverance crowd views sickness as either natural or given by God for His sovereign purposes. Rarely are health issues considered to be demonic, even though Scripture provides examples of demons causing sickness. The only answer to sickness becomes medicine or the skill of doctors and other health professionals.

The Groundhogs

Two animals that illustrate these two extremes are the groundhog and the ostrich. The groundhog is a skittish creature that seems to be afraid of its own shadow. Like the groundhog, hyperdeliverance folks can seem afraid of their own humanity. They blame human frailties on demons. If they have a lustful thought, it is the work of demons. If they overspend and blow their budgets, a spirit of poverty has descended on them, making it hard to pay their bills.

Should they have an argument with their spouses, they call the minister, asking him to drive the demons out of their homes. They experience repeated problems, so they blame their problems on a curse someone put on them.

A woman called me up sounding desperate. "My husband is under a curse that his ex-wife put on him."

I began to inquire as to how she knew he had demons.

"It's simple. My husband has fallen in love with his ex-wife and wants to leave me."

"Sometimes that happens," I said, "but it may not necessarily be a curse that is put on him."

She was unable to explain why she thought it was a curse. She merely assumed that anything bad that happened in her life had to be the work of demons or came through a curse. The more I inquired about her situation, the more I realized that this woman, sincere though she was, had made the common mistake of blaming demons for all her earthly problems.

She even admitted that infidelity was not new to her husband. "My husband and I met when he was married to that Jezebel! I was able to save him from the floozy."

"Wait a minute," I said. "Are you saying that you both started an affair while he was still married?"

She paused for a moment, then said, "Well, uh, yeah. But this woman is not good for him."

I then corrected her, "Listen, you had no right to break up a marriage. I don't think your husband has any demons that were brought on by his ex-wife. What you need to know is how wrong you have been. You need to take responsibility for your actions."

As much as this woman wanted to blame her problems on demons, what she really needed was to take responsibility for her own actions and allow her husband to take responsibility for his.

I would be a rich man if I had a dollar for every phone call I have received from someone who was sure that all his problems in life were the result of some sort of curse. Sometimes the curse was from a mean relative or fellow worker. Other times it was from an ex-spouse. Rarely is there a realization of personal responsibility. Someone—or something—else is always to blame!

I have never seen a person improve and grow in the Lord while, at the same time, blaming his problems on curses.

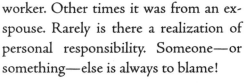

Even when some of these people are right about the curse, they often ascribe more power to the demons and curses in their lives than to the Holy Spirit. I ask you: Who is greater, the devil in others or God in you? Let us believe the greater One inside of us. Let us take authority over any curses we think people have placed on us and stop dwelling on them. I have never seen a person improve and grow in the Lord while, at the same time, blaming his problems on curses.

Years ago, our family was going to move into our first home, but the deal fell through. We filed a lawsuit to make a claim for the money we had spent to paint the house. The owner countered that because we had supposedly reneged on the deal, she had lost money that could have been made by renting the house. To prove the house was rented quickly, I went to the new tenants and asked them when they had moved into the house. Their answer clearly showed that the house was rented right away.

They asked, "Why do you want to know?"

I explained that we were supposed to be tenants in the house, but that the deal did not materialize. When I said that, the eyes of the new tenants got big.

"Are you Pastor Tom Brown?"

"Yes."

"Wait right there!" The lady went into the house and brought out a postcard, saying, "This postcard was sent to you. Look, it says, 'Welcome to our neighborhood, from the Satanists of El Paso.'"

I laughed.

"This is not funny," the lady exclaimed. "They think you live here."

I assured her that there was nothing to fear.

If a hyperdeliverance person had received that card, he would have been paralyzed with fear. He would be constantly on the lookout for all manner of trouble coming his way. If anything happened, you can be sure he would lay the blame for his trouble on the door of the Satanists.

I brushed it off, however, because I knew that greater was He who was in me than he who was in the world.

(See 1 John 4:4.) I had faith that God would protect me from harm.

How Do I Know I'm Free?

"Pastor, I have been through several deliverance sessions, and I'm told by my minister that most of the demons have gone, but there are still some more left. How will I know they have all left me?"

This question shows an inherent weakness in the candidate. He is buying into the idea that demons are stronger than God. If he truly believes the gospel, the minister who prayed for him would have driven out *all* the demons, not just a *few*. Such lingering doubts give room for Satan to continue his work.

Why would any demons stay inside of a believer? It's easier to believe that demons might remain in a sinner who has not fully submitted himself to the claims of Christ, but how can demons continue to remain inside a believer when the command for them to leave has already been made? Satan loves it when people doubt the power of the Holy Spirit. When this happens, he is able to make himself appear as strong as God in the eyes of the saints. This is a terrible and unhealthy view to take.

Satan loves it when people doubt the power of the Holy Spirit.

As long as you remain confused about your full authority in Christ, you will always struggle with your faith. No amount of deliverance will help. I often refuse to pray for people who are "chronic" seekers of deliverance. In my experience, their problem is due not to the strength of demons but to the weakness of their faith. Their faith is weak because they have not fed it with the Word of God. God's Word will give you everything you need to overcome all the power of Satan.

The Ostriches

Be self-controlled and alert. Your enemy the devil prowls around like a roaring lion looking for someone to devour. (1 Peter 5:8)

Those in the nondeliverance crowd often remind me of the ostrich, a bird that is said to stick its head in the sand because it is afraid to confront an enemy. Avoiding confrontation in this way only gives "a hungry lion" an easy lunch. The nondeliverance crowd does not see how responsible Satan is for a lot of the problems in the world. Consider the story of the first sin. Try to read it afresh, as if it is the first time you've read it. Get rid of your preconceived notions about God confronting the first couple's sin.

Then the man and his wife heard the sound of the LORD God as he was walking in the garden in the cool of the day, and they hid from the LORD God among the trees of the garden. But the LORD God called to the man, "Where are you?" He answered, "I heard you in the garden, and I was afraid because I was naked; so I hid." And he said, "Who told you that you were naked? Have you eaten from the tree that I commanded you not to eat from?" The man said, "The woman you put here with me—she gave me some fruit from the tree, and I ate it." Then

> the LORD God said to the woman, "What is this
> you have done?" The woman said, "The serpent
> deceived me, and I ate."   (Genesis 3:8–13)

All too often, I have heard ministers use this story to show that we cannot blame anyone but ourselves for our sin. Yet a careful reading of the story proves the opposite. Adam admitted to eating the fruit, but he pointed out the obvious fact that Eve gave the fruit to him. In other words, she was also accountable for the temptation. God did not rebuke Adam for blaming his wife; rather, He turned to the woman and said, "What is this you have done?" God seemed to agree with Adam concerning the culpability of Eve. Most theologians seem to disagree with Adam's approach, yet Adam was correct in attributing part of the blame to the woman.

It is true that most of our problems stem from our fleshly nature, but Satan is always working fervently on our flesh to drag us away from God.

Next, Eve confirmed that she did eat, but she blamed the serpent for deceiving her. Did God reprimand her for "passing the buck" to the serpent? No, He turned His attention to the serpent and cursed him. Notice that He did not ask the serpent any of the same questions. He never let the serpent make an excuse. The reason is simple: the devil had no one to blame but himself. For Adam and Eve, there were some extenuating circumstances in part to explain why they ate the forbidden fruit. Others had enticed them to disobey God.

I bring this up because many people in the nondeliverance camp refuse to see the role Satan plays in temptation. They would rather view temptation as simply something we all "naturally" go through, rather than as the plot of an adversary who tempts us supernaturally. It is true that most of our problems stem from our fleshly nature, but Satan is always working fervently on our flesh to drag us away from God. It is not just a matter of being weak, but also a matter of our adversary taking advantage of our weaknesses.

Paul

Paul was a handsome young man who taught a weekly Bible study at his church. Despite looking like he had everything together, there was a deep sinking feeling in his life. Suffering from depression since he was a child, Paul would often withdraw from other people. As a teen, Paul often skipped school and avoided hanging out with friends. As an adult, he withdrew from his wife and children, sometimes disappearing from the family for days. His wife loved him, but she couldn't explain his strange behavior.

One day, Paul was invited to come to our church where I was speaking on the spirit of depression. His pastor had never dealt with Paul's need for deliverance, but the more he heard me talk about it, the more he realized that this was exactly what Paul needed. When I laid hands on Paul and spoke to the spirit of depression, Paul began to scream. The spirit in him yelled, "No, no. Stop it. Quit yelling at me! He is mine! I am not going to leave him!"

"What is your name?" I commanded.

Paul's voice spoke, "I am the spirit of depression."

"I command the spirit of depression to come out of this man!"

Paul plummeted to the ground. After a few minutes, he stood up, dazed, then looked at me and smiled. "I feel so good," he said. "It's like a hundred-pound weight has been removed from my shoulders!"

Later he told me that he blanked out when I began to pray for him. I told him what had happened, as well as what the demon had said through his voice. He was shocked.

"Nothing like this has ever happened to me."

There are many people like Paul in churches today. They seem confident on the outside, but inside there are spiritual battles going on that have never been won—battles that won't be won until the church recognizes the role of deliverance.

Recently I visited a member of my congregation in the hospital. She was new to the church, and her mother had requested that I visit her. She had been in and out of mental institutions during the previous year. When I arrived, she was in a psychotic state. I gently laid hands on her to pray for her. She reacted fiercely, growled, and thrust my hand off her head. I did not stop praying, and, after a few minutes, she improved and came out of her psychotic state.

Finally, the doctor arrived. The girl's mother told the doctor that it was all right to reveal his diagnosis in front of me. The doctor sat down, examined the charts, then looked up and said, "We have run all sorts of tests, and it shows that there is nothing physically wrong with your daughter. There is nothing we can do for her." Then, the doctor looked at me and said, "What your daughter needs is him."

Even this doctor recognized that there were inexplicable things for which doctors and medicine had no cure. The daughter greatly improved after my visit. She has not been cured completely, but she is making great progress toward normalcy.

The following chart describes the differences between the hyperdeliverance and nondeliverance groups.

Hyperdeliverance	Nondeliverance
1. Views God and Satan as equals.	1. Views Satan as irrelevant to God and the believer.
2. Believes all problems stem directly from Satan.	2. Believes all problems stem directly from the sovereign hand of God.
3. Blames curses as the constant source of problems.	3. Sees the idea of curses as being totally superstitious.
4. Thinks nearly everyone, to a certain degree, has demons.	4. Thinks no one has demons.
5. Doubts that one can totally be rid of demons.	5. Doubts that anyone really is inhabited by demons.

Hyperdeliverance	Nondeliverance
6. Looks to deliverance as the best way to pursue sanctification.	6. Looks to deliverance as a bad way to pursue sanctification.
7. Seeks freedom but never seems to attain it.	7. Never seeks freedom but instead gives the appearance of peace.
8. Looks at powerful encounters as the main technique of deliverance.	8. Looks at encounters with truth as the only legitimate technique of deliverance.

Two Methods of Driving Out Demons

There are two important biblical methods of driving out demons: power encounters and truth encounters. A power encounter is the exercise of the power of the Spirit released by the minister, giving an order for the demons to leave. Often there are physical manifestations with this method, including screaming, growling, and falling down.

A truth encounter uses the truth of Scripture to help a candidate know his position and rights as a child of God. This method is more subdued and helps the candidate to refocus on his position and rights in Christ. We need to maintain a balance in this area of deliverance by practicing both methods.

Unfortunately, the power encounter is the only method the hyperdeliverance minister takes, while the truth encounter is the only method the nondeliverance minister takes. The true deliverance minister understands that both methods are necessary. When it comes to ministering to a chronic seeker of deliverance, I refuse to use power encounters; instead, I use only truth encounters. I find it useless to pray the same deliverance prayers over and over again. The chronic seeker of deliverance needs to accept all the benefits of his redemption or there will be no permanent relief for his issues. On top of this, he needs to realize that there are three battles to overcome: the flesh, the world, and the devil. Unfortunately, this person tends to ignore the first two battles, focusing only on the battle with the devil.

The chronic seeker of deliverance needs to accept all the benefits of redemption or there will be no permanent relief.

You can't win the battle over the flesh by concentrating on the devil. And for chronic deliverance seekers, it is often the flesh that is their enemy, not actually the devil.

Chapter Eight

How to Overcome the Flesh

Nick suffered a great deal from breathing problems due to his addiction to cigarettes. It was his desire to break free from this habit. He had heard about my deliverance ministry, and he came to me fully expecting to be delivered from the spirit of nicotine. The Lord, however, led me to talk with Nick about the role the flesh plays in keeping people bound. I explained that some of our problems can be overcome only by subjecting the flesh, not by removing demons.

A light went off in Nick's spirit. He realized that he was not suffering from a demon but simply a bad habit that could be solved by overcoming his flesh. Nick came forward for prayer—not to be delivered from demons, but to ask for strength to overcome his addiction to cigarettes. Today, Nick is tobacco free.

Some believers do not seem to grasp the reality that we face three adversaries: the flesh, the world, and the devil.

> *For all that is in the world, the lust of the flesh, and the lust of the eyes, and the pride of life, is not of the Father, but is of the world.* (1 John 2:16 KJV)

You can rid your body of demons, but you cannot eliminate the appetites of the body.

The flesh lusts. The flesh is related to the appetites of our bodies. Adam and Eve had an appetite for the forbidden fruit, but their appetite was not caused by demons. You can rid your body of demons, but you cannot eliminate the appetites of the body. Thus, even if someone is delivered from a demon, he still has the responsibility of winning the battle with his flesh.

Putting Off the Old Self

A woman once cried out to me, "Pastor, please pray that God removes all the sinful desires I have."

I began to pray for her, "Dear Lord, would You please take Your daughter home to heaven so she won't have any bad desires anymore."

Shocked at my prayer, she backed away. "Pastor Brown, why are you praying that I die?"

"Sister, the only way you will never have sinful desires is for you to die. In this world, you will always have sinful desires, but you need to learn to not act on them."

She laughed as she understood my point.

The apostle Paul explained what believers must to do with their sinful desires:

> *You were taught, with regard to your former way of life, to put off your old self, which is being corrupted by its deceitful desires; to be made new in the attitude of your minds; and to put on the new self,*

> *created to be like God in true righteousness and*
> *holiness.*   (Ephesians 4:22–24)

Paul never mentioned a need for deliverance. He simply said to the believer, *"put off your old self."* The old self is the flesh. Hyperdeliverance people, however, consider the old self to be demons. They reason that anything sinful must be attributed to demons.

Paul had a more practical and workable solution for believers who struggled with worldly temptation—they were to shelve the old desires. God says to put your flesh under subjection to His Spirit. Do not give in to the appetites of the flesh. If you are prone to overeating, God has an answer: *"Put a knife to your throat if you are given to gluttony"* (Proverbs 23:2).

It is much easier to cast out a demon than it is to deny the flesh.

Believe it or not, it is much easier to cast out a demon than it is to deny the flesh. Besides, if someone believes that he needs deliverance, then he is not to blame for his sin. The bottom line: a person who thinks he is demon possessed is often someone who is not exercising self-control.

Breaking Addictions

We live in a society that seems overcome by addictions. Everyone appears to be addicted to something. Many professionals have jumped on the bandwagon by promising solutions to every human condition—overeating, alcohol abuse, tobacco habits, gambling, drug addiction, pornography, and a host of other life-controlling problems. Despite the countless solutions offered, however, countless people are not getting better.

The Holy Spirit gave you self-control, but it is hard to exercise without growing in the knowledge of God.

Why do so many remain enslaved to addictions? Perhaps it is because many of the promised remedies ignore or downplay the real solution: *you.* Yes, the solution to your compulsive behavior may be you!

No matter what controls you, you can crush those insurmountable habits that hold you in their clutches! How? Through self-control!

Almost everyone agrees that we need to have self-control, but few understand how to practice it. Many believe that self-control is not within their nature. While that may be true, it is possible for those who are born again. The Bible says that self-control is a gift of the Holy Spirit for the believer:

> *But the fruit of the Spirit is love, joy, peace, patience, kindness, goodness, faithfulness, gentleness and self-control.* (Galatians 5:22–23)

As a believer, you need to grow in your self-control. A child is born with legs, but he can't walk until he grows. The same is true of self-control. The Holy Spirit gave you self-control, but it is hard to exercise it without growing in the knowledge of God. Let me explain.

Knowledge Produces Self-control

One of the main passages that deals with self-control is found in 2 Peter:

> *His divine power has given us **everything** we need for life and godliness through our knowledge of him who called us by his own glory and goodness. Through these he has given us his very great and precious promises, so that through them you may participate in the divine nature and escape the corruption in the world caused by evil desires.*
>
> (2 Peter 1:3–4, emphasis added)

Isn't that what you desire, to *"escape the corruption in the world* [alcohol abuse, gambling, drug addiction, gluttony, etc.] *caused by evil desires?"* How do you escape these things? The next verses reveal the answer:

> *For this very reason, make every effort to add to your faith goodness; and to goodness, knowledge; and to knowledge, self-control; and to self-control, perseverance; and to perseverance, godliness; and to godliness, brotherly kindness; and to brotherly kindness, love.* (verses 5–7)

To have true self-control, you must first accept Jesus Christ as your Savior, which will make you a partaker of God's divine nature. Self-control is one of the attributes of God. He will give it to those who are born again.

But self-control is not fully matured at conversion. First, there is faith, but you must add to that *all* the virtues of God's divine nature: goodness, knowledge, self-control, perseverance, godliness, brotherly kindness, and love. Notice that Peter did not give us a haphazard list of virtues; instead, he gave us a progressive list of Christian qualities that produce continuous growth. Look carefully at the list and notice how each virtue gives birth to another—each in its respective order.

Knowledge precedes self-control; in fact, it actually leads to self-control.

It is similar to the growth of a child. A child does not speak, read, write, walk, and run all on the same day. Rather, the child picks an easy ability and uses it until he is proficient at it. Later, he is ready to exercise another ability, and so on. Before a child can read, he must learn to speak. Speaking always precedes reading. In the same way, self-control cannot be practiced unless there is another virtue that has matured in you.

What virtue must you have? In the midst of this list, Peter said, "*and to knowledge,* [add] *self-control*" (verse 6). Knowledge precedes self-control; in fact, it actually leads to self-control. This isn't just any knowledge, but the knowledge of God.

Knowing the Truth Sets You Free

If knowledge is essential in order to have self-control, then we can assume that the opposite of knowledge—a lack of it, or ignorance—destroys self-control. The lack of knowledge could also be called a firm belief in false information.

Jesus said, *"Then you will know the truth, and the truth will set you free"* (John 8:32). What sets you free? Knowing the truth does. Not truth alone, but *knowing* the truth, liberates you. The opposite is also true: lies will keep you bound. Jesus called Satan the *"father of lies"* (John 8:44). Satan will tell any lie that he can to keep you bound in sin and harmful habits.

According to the apostle James, if we speak lies to ourselves, our bodies become uncontrollable. *"We all stumble in many ways. If anyone is never at fault in what he says, he is a perfect man, able to keep his whole body in check"* (James 3:2). James was telling us that the person who speaks the truth is in control of himself; in other words, he is *self*-controlled. When we speak lies, even to ourselves, we lose that control. Such lies can come in the form of wrong beliefs. These lies must be replaced with the truth.

Lies We Believe

One of the main lies we tell ourselves in order to avoid exercising self-control is this: *Since I've failed before, I'll always fail.* Yet, experience tells us that most people who have overcome hurtful habits had to make many attempts to break their habits—including many failed attempts. Most ex-smokers try to give up cigarettes numerous times before they are finally able to give them up permanently. Failing in the past does not guarantee failing in the future!

Another common lie we believe that can halt self-control is: *I'm only hurting myself.* Those who believe this lie have never been counselors. I have counseled dozens of wives who were heartbroken over their wrecked marriages, their lives in shambles because their intoxicated husbands wouldn't stop drinking. Their flooding tears testified to the fact that sin hurts not just the offenders, but everyone around them.

Some people believe this lie to avoid feelings of guilt over their actions. The damage that sin produces, however, is not restricted to the sinner alone—there is collateral damage, as well.

> *Despite the lies that Satan tells, you can endure the pain of self-denial. You will survive. You really will!*

Here is another lie we swallow: *I can't deny myself.* Jesus said, *"If anyone would come after me, he must deny himself and take up his cross and follow me"* (Matthew 16:24). He obviously believed that people had the power to deny themselves. If He didn't, it would have been extremely unfair to demand such self-denial of His followers.

"But you don't understand my situation."

"My temptation is more than I can handle!"

"I can't take the pressure!"

Yet God said, *"No temptation has seized you except what is common to man. And God is faithful; he will not let you be tempted beyond what you can bear"* (1 Corinthians 10:13). God won't allow you to be tempted beyond what you can handle; you have the capability of resisting any tempting action or behavior.

In truth, some people simply don't want to have to endure temptation, but they can—if they choose to. You *can* say "no" to yourself. Despite the lies that Satan tells, you can endure the pain of self-denial. You will survive. You really will!

Do you like ice cream?

"Yes," you may say, "I love ice cream. That's my weakness. I cannot say 'no' to ice cream."

"Yes, in fact, you can."

"Oh, no, I can't. I love it too much."

Allow me to prove that you can say "no" to ice cream.

Imagine yourself inside the largest ice cream parlor in the world. Inside is every flavor imaginable—more than your greatest fantasy could ever conceive. The clerk behind the counter asks, "What would you like? Name it and I'll make it for you." You give the clerk your order, and he promptly makes the largest, creamiest ice cream delight that you have ever seen. The clerk hands it to you, along with a large spoon.

Here's my question: Can you put down that ice cream?

"Oh, no! I can't!"

Let's add something else to the story. As you are about to put a heaping spoonful into your mouth, you hear a click as you feel a cold, metal object touch your head. Out of the corner of your left eye, you catch a glimpse of a large hand holding a gun to your temple. A deep voice warns, "If you eat that ice cream, I'll blow your head off!"

Let me ask that question again: Can you put down that ice cream?

I think you see the point: you can say "no" if you understand the consequences.

"The wages [consequence] *of sin is death"* (Romans 6:23). Sin destroys your life.

Resisting temptation is worth it!

It is not easy to deny yourself, but for the sake of having a higher, nobler life, it is necessary. Most of the time, you will find that gaining something valuable in your life will depend on your willingness to tolerate distress, discomfort, and discontent. This is what Paul meant when he wrote, *"We also rejoice in our sufferings, because we know that suffering produces perseverance; perseverance, character; and character, hope"* (Romans 5:3–4). Resisting temptation is worth it!

Thoughts Are Not Deeds

Another lie we tell ourselves is: *Since I thought it, I might as well do it.* This lie is usually associated with lustful thoughts. People usually misinterpret Jesus's teaching on adultery, which was, *"But I tell you that anyone who looks at a woman lustfully has already committed adultery with her in his heart"* (Matthew 5:28).

Some will claim, "Well, since thinking about it is the same as doing it, I might as well do it." This rationale would be funny if it were not so tragic. If thinking about something is the same as doing it, why do you ever need to do it? It's clear that thinking lustful thoughts is not the same as actually acting on them.

Look carefully at what Jesus said concerning a man who lusts for another woman besides his wife. He said that such a man has *"committed adultery with her in his heart."* Notice that He did not say that the man committed adultery in his flesh. Adultery in the heart is wrong, but it is not equal to adultery in the flesh. First of all, try using this rationale with your wife and see if she buys it. "Honey, since I have already thought lustful thoughts about someone, I'm going to go ahead and pursue her, since I am already guilty."

I'll be surprised if she doesn't set you straight!

You can desire cigarettes all day long, but you won't get lung cancer by thinking about them. You will have to smoke them to bring physical harm to your body. Thoughts are not the same as deeds.

Another lie we tell ourselves is: *I've worked so hard and done so well, so I deserve to indulge a little bit.*

Jesus told us to adopt a more humble attitude when we have done well, saying,

> *So you also, when you have done everything you were told to do, should say, "We are unworthy servants; we have only done our duty."*
>
> (Luke 17:10)

Many people try to reward themselves for doing their reasonable duty by actually undoing the good they have done. A husband who had been addicted to gambling almost lost everything, so he finally stopped gambling for an entire year. One day, he came home holding two flight tickets to

Las Vegas. "Honey, look!" he told his wife. "I haven't gambled in more than a year. It won't hurt to go for the weekend."

This man believed he deserved to splurge. What he failed to realize was that the moment he entered the casino, the gambling bug would hit him again.

Another lie we tell ourselves is: *I really need this.*

This person has confused a *need* with a *desire.* You don't *need* an extra piece of pie. You don't *need* to go to the strip club. You don't *need* to snort cocaine. What you are really trying to say is you *desire* and *lust* for it. You don't really *need* it to survive.

Someone might say, "That's right, I don't need it; I can give it up anytime, I just don't want to." What a joke! This person does not "want to" because lust has overtaken him. He doesn't want to admit that he is being *controlled.*

"*Those controlled by the sinful nature cannot please God*" (Romans 8:8). This person does not want to admit that something evil controls him. Until he admits this, he will never seek to put his flesh under subjection.

Finally, another big lie we tell ourselves is: *Someone else made me do it.*

A husband argues, "My wife got me so angry; it is her fault for making me hit her." No one has control over your actions but you. Others may make excuses: "You don't understand—I couldn't help but steal because of the neighborhood I grew up in." I am sorry that you did not have the best circumstances growing up, but even those circumstances cannot *make* you do anything. Other people have had similar circumstances, yet they resisted the temptation to be thieves. You can, too.

The Stage Is Set

Self-control is a choice. You can choose how your life is going to be.

You may argue. "I didn't choose to be an alcoholic. It's not my fault that I grew up with alcoholic parents. If I hadn't had them as parents, I wouldn't be an alcoholic today."

Please, don't confuse what others did with what you are doing. They are responsible for their lives, but you are responsible for yours.

Life is like a stage play. You come on the scene with the stage already set. You did not choose your setting. You did not choose the parents who may have abused you. You did not select the teachers at school who ridiculed you. You did not pick out the peers who teased you. You did not desire a spouse who cheated on you. You did not pick the stage, set, and props. They were here when you arrived, or perhaps they changed without your consent.

Self-control is a choice. You can choose how your life is going to be.

God comes to you, however, with a blank piece of paper in His hands. He gives it to you, along with a pen. Then, He says to you, in effect, "The stage is already set, but you must write the script. You will choose what your character will do in this real-life play. You will decide how your character will react to the parents, friends, and acquaintances you have."

In your life's drama, you determine how you will respond to ridiculing teachers or teasing peers. You determine what you are going to do after your spouse leaves you for another person. Are you going to wallow in self-pity, drown your sorrows in the bottle, or gorge yourself with food? Or, will you forgive and make your life better? The choice is yours. You—and you alone—write the script!

A deliverance minister does not have the power to write your script. It is called *self*-control for a reason; you are the only person who can implement it. Only you have the ability to exercise it. Do not tell yourself that you cannot do it. That is a lie!

The script is in your hands. You're the author. What will you write?

Part Three

Spiritual Warfare

Chapter Nine

What Are Fallen Angels?

Most people who hear my teachings inevitably want to know the difference between demons and fallen angels. It is the purpose of this chapter to explain the characteristics of fallen angels and their work as well as to clarify the difference between them and their fellow worker demons.

1. Fallen Angels Live in Heavenly Places

Paul described two types of spiritual entities:

> *Finally, be strong in the Lord and in his mighty power. Put on the full armor of God so that you can take your stand against the devil's schemes. For our struggle is not against flesh and blood, but against the rulers, against the authorities, against the powers of this dark world and against the spiritual forces of evil in the heavenly realms.*

(Ephesians 6:10–12)

This simple truth is often overlooked. Here we read of two locations for evil entities: *"powers of this dark world"* and *"spiritual forces of evil in the heavenly realms."* Some spirits dwell in this world, while others reside in the heavenlies. It is my belief that fallen angels reside in the heavenlies, while demons dwell on the earth.

While it is true that Satan's angels were kicked out of heaven when they joined in the rebellion against God, the heaven they were expelled from was the *"third heaven"* (2 Corinthians 12:2), where God dwells. If there is a third heaven, it would only be logical to assume that there must also be a first and second heaven, at least. The *"heavenly realms"* mentioned in Ephesians are actually the "second heaven." Just because God expelled the angels from heaven, however, does not mean that He clipped their wings.

The devil has an organized, underhanded plot against each person, church, city, and nation.

Unlike angels, demons are never described as winged creatures, and they seem to be limited to the earth. The demons inside the madman of Gadara pleaded with Jesus not to send them out of the area. (See Mark 5:10.) Their only choice was limited to roaming the earth. They could not fly away into the heavenlies. In fact, Jesus said that when a demon is cast out, *"he walketh through dry places"* (Matthew 12:43 KJV). Although it could be argued that the Greek word for *walketh* carries a different meaning from "to walk on foot," the point is that demons go through dry places—a term that seems to indicate land. They do not fly off into the sky but continue to wander through the land. Fallen angels, on the other hand, live in the heavenly places.

In a military sense (since we are in a spiritual war), demons would resemble the army, while fallen angels would represent the air force. The air force is a greater threat and has greater striking power than a ground army. An air force will almost always defeat ground troops. In the same way, fallen angels, by their shear ability to fly, have greater power and authority than demons.

2. Fallen Angels Are under the Rule of the Devil

Both demons and fallen angels are controlled by Satan, who is also referred to as the *"prince of demons"* (Matthew 9:34), so it's clear that he rules over demons. The same is true of fallen angels. They are actually called Satan's angels. (See Revelation 12:7.) They are ruled by a spiritual dictator and do not act on their own without direct orders from Satan.

When Paul described the rulers, authorities, powers, and spiritual forces of evil, he said, *"Put on the full armor of God so that you can take your stand against the devil's schemes"* (Ephesians 6:11). The work of these spiritual entities is to carry out *"the devil's schemes."*

Make no mistake about it, the devil has an organized, underhanded plot against each person, church, city, and nation. Fallen angels labor to carry out his scheme. They do not work haphazardly but use careful planning. Just as the military is highly organized—having detailed plans and a distinct hierarchy, from generals to privates—so, too, Satan has an organized force of evil to help him carry out his diabolical work.

3. Fallen Angels Have Maintained Their Celestial Form

Contrary to how they are portrayed in classic medieval artwork, fallen angels did not mutate into grotesque, monster-like creatures resembling insects, fearsome animals, or deformed men. Demons may have some of those features, but not fallen angels. Demons are a particular class of beings while fallen angels are quite another.

The Bible describes their nature:

> Bold and arrogant, these men are not afraid to slander celestial beings; yet even angels, although they are stronger and more powerful, do not bring slanderous accusations against such beings in the presence of the Lord. (2 Peter 2:10–11)

Why are angels careful about slandering their fallen comrades? Despite their fallen state, these angels are still *"celestial beings." Celestial* means "heavenly." As I noted earlier, fallen angels still live in the heavenlies among God's angels.

The word *celestial* also speaks to the type of bodies these angels have. We humans have "terrestrial" bodies—physical, tangible bodies made from the earth. Although we have a spirit within, we operate in the material realm. We have the ability to influence the spiritual realm only through the power of God's Spirit. Without God's Spirit working through us, we would be unable to influence, cast out, or drive away fallen angels. The primary world we control is the physical one.

Angels, on the other hand, have bodies made up of spirit; in fact, they are called spirits. An angelic spirit is capable of operating in two realms—the spiritual and the physical. Most people will acknowledge that angels operate in the spiritual realm, but many are surprised to discover that they can also operate in the physical realm. The Bible says that angels fed Elijah (see 1 Kings 19:5, 7), opened the prison doors for the apostles to escape (see Acts 5:19), and protected Daniel from harm by physically shutting the mouths of the lions. (See Daniel 6:22.)

Demons, on the other hand, do not perform physical acts. They cannot move furniture, open doors, or levitate people. Since fallen angels have celestial bodies, however, they are able to manipulate the physical world. It is my view that so-called "haunted houses" are primarily the work of fallen angels, not demons.

Most people will acknowledge that angels operate in the spiritual realm, but many are surprised to discover that they can also operate in the physical realm.

Mark and Debbie lived in a haunted house in which they experienced strange things, from unusual noises to levitating objects. They even saw a female "ghost figure" roaming their home. They tried many things to get rid of this spirit, but nothing worked. They sprinkled their house with holy water and even erected a huge cross on their roof, yet the spirit would not leave. It was not until they started attending my church that they learned that, in their authority as children of God, they could rebuke spirits and cast them out. After learning this great truth, they took authority and banished the evil angel from their home, at which time the entire strange phenomenon stopped.

Although fallen angels retain their celestial form, they do not have the moral compass of God's angels. They do not desire to obey God or do what is right, because their minds have been corrupted.

4. Fallen Angels Affect the Atmosphere of the World

> *As for you, you were dead in your transgressions and sins, in which you used to live when you followed the ways of this world and of the ruler of the kingdom of the air, the spirit who is now at work in those who are disobedient.*
>
> (Ephesians 2:1–2)

Satan is called *"the ruler of the kingdom of the air."* There is arrayed in the air a highly organized enemy force, which works to cause the unsaved to follow the ways of this world. The word *air* refers to the lowest of spiritual heavens. The

Fallen angels work to create an atmosphere for demons to do their work.

term also means "atmosphere." Fallen angels work to create an atmosphere for demons to do their diabolical work. Similar to an air force, they fly over a territory and provide covering for the ground troops to succeed at their job. Fallen angels create the right political, social, religious, and philosophical environment that enables demons to personally control people in their surroundings. One word describes this atmosphere: *culture*. Fallen angels create a culture that makes it difficult for people to get saved or for believers to follow Christ wholeheartedly.

People often ask me if certain cities or locations have more demons than others, and the quick answer is *yes*. Where fallen angels have had success, there will be more demonic activity. That is why it is essential that we correctly wage effective warfare against these spiritual forces of evil in the heavenly realms.

5. Fallen Angels May Do Some of the Activities of Demons

Just because demons and fallen angels are different from one another does not mean that a clear line of demarcation separates these beings. Fallen angels do some of the things that demons do. The devil is also called *"the tempter"* (Matthew 4:3, 1 Thessalonians 3:5), and he is an angel. Therefore, fallen angels can still tempt us.

The primary meaning of the word *angel* is "messenger." A messenger's job is to convey a message or word from another. An angel does not need to materialize in order to give us a message. For example, Scripture tells us that Philip heard the voice of an angel.

> *Now an angel of the Lord said to Philip, "Go south to the road—the desert road—that goes down from Jerusalem to Gaza."* (Acts 8:26)

It does not seem like an angel materialized; it simply spoke to him. I am personally convinced that many of the thoughts and ideas we have come from the voices of angels, as they did for Philip. When we have good thoughts and divine ideas, they may have come from God's angels; on the other hand, when we have bad thoughts and devilish ideas, they may have come from Satan's fallen angels.

The great theologian Thomas Aquinas wrote, "An angel can illuminate the thought and mind of man by strengthening the power of vision." I agree with him. Likewise, I believe that a fallen angel can "darken" the thought and mind of man by "diminishing" man's vision of God.

Satan's angels also stir up problems by tempting others to persecute Christians. Paul's thorn in the flesh was an apt example: "*To keep me from becoming conceited because of these surpassingly great revelations, there was given me a thorn in*

Evil angels are more difficult to remove than demons.

my flesh, a messenger of Satan, to torment me" (2 Corinthians 12:7). Paul clearly demonstrated that messengers, or angels, from Satan can torment a believer. I am aware of the different interpretations of what the "thorn" actually did to Paul, but it is my view that the thorn aroused great persecution for him. He described

the effects of the thorn in these words: "*That is why, for Christ's sake, I delight in weaknesses, in insults, in hardships, in persecutions, in difficulties. For when I am weak, then I am strong*" (2 Corinthians 12:10).

Paul was indicating that this evil angel kept stirring up persecution wherever he went. These persecutions kept Paul from being able to share the revelations God had given him. Paul's response to this fallen angel was to pray to God: *"Three times I pleaded with the Lord to take it away from me. But he said to me, 'My grace is sufficient for you, for my power is made perfect in weakness'"* (verses 8–9). Paul's method of dealing with persecution by fallen angels was prayer. Often, we get the idea that all we need to do is rebuke an evil angel and send it on its way. I wish it were that easy. Evil angels are more difficult to remove than demons.

6. Fallen Angels Are Not Easily Removed from a Person, a Church, an Area, or a Nation

Our work to overcome fallen angels requires great effort. Though we may confront them directly in the name of Jesus, we must often employ additional weapons to overcome their effect. A soldier typically needs only a machine gun or a rifle to combat enemy ground soldiers. When attacked from the air, however, the soldier's weapon has little effectiveness.

Daniel prayed and fasted for twenty-one days before he saw the *"prince of Persia"* (a fallen angel) pushed back from destroying Israel. (See Daniel 10:13.)

Consider Judas Iscariot. The Bible says, *"Satan entered into him"* (John 13:27). Judas died in this state. When evil angels are at work in a person, a church, or a nation, it will often take more than a simple rebuke to remove them. They are strong beings and will not be easily dislodged from their assignment.

In contrast, demons are relatively easy to drive out with a simple order. When MSNBC filmed one of my deliverance services in our church, they commented, "In less than five minutes, the deliverance was over." It surprised them that deliverance could occur in such a short time. Of course, I was not dealing with a fallen angel in this case, but a demon. A fallen angel would not be removed from a person so quickly.

In most of the cases I have witnessed, fallen angels will not enter a person, because to do so would limit their movement. As mentioned before, angels—fallen or otherwise—have their own celestial bodies and do not need the bodies of humans to manifest themselves. Gabriel did not *need* to take over a human body to appear before Mary or Zacharias. In a case such as Judas, however, Satan found it advantageous to enter into a human form. (See Luke 22:3.) When this happens, it will take much prayer, fasting, and discernment to drive an angel from the person.

In most cases, the assignment of certain high-ranking angels will not involve just one person, but a group of people.

In most cases, it seems that the assignment of certain high-ranking angels will not involve just one person, but a group of people—be it a church, a city, an area, or a nation. Just as there are angels over churches, as the book of Revelation mentions (see, for example, Revelation 2:1), there are also evil angels attempting to exercise their influence over churches.

Ruben has been a member of my church for two decades. He is not easily given to visions, but he once told me, "Tom, I was driving my car when I saw an angel flying. I began to follow it wherever it went. It eventually took me to Word of Life Church." Both good and bad angels really do have assignments over churches, cities, and nations.

7. Fallen Angels Are Defeated Only through Intense Spiritual Warfare

"For the weapons of our warfare are not carnal, but mighty through God to the pulling down of strongholds" (2 Corinthians 10:4 KJV). This passage has been twisted and abused to imply that we can simply "pull down" angelic forces of the heavenly realms. The active verbal phrase *"pulling down"* has fueled the imaginations of many believers, causing them to visualize fallen angels in the heavenlies as being "shot down" by rebukes. They will say something like, "In the name of Jesus, I pull down the strongholds in heavenly places." In their minds, they create a dramatic scene in which their commands are like cruise missiles, fired at the angels, that send them plummeting to earth like so many enemy fighter jets in war movies, or, at the very least, driving them from the territory in which they ruled.

Some praying saints have taken spiritual warfare to even greater lengths by actually renting helicopters to get a little closer to the battlefield in the sky. From there, they launch shouts of victory, commanding the "territorial spirits" to leave the region. They are convinced that the spirits will leave at their command.

There is one problem with this tactic: it doesn't work! After all these efforts at spiritual warfare and "claiming cities for Christ," these areas remain unchanged. Bars remain open. Nightclubs are packed. Divorce rates continue to skyrocket. Abortion mills are still slaughtering the unborn. Crime, corruption, and injustice continue. Churches are in decline. It seems that, with all this warfare, we should have seen better results than this.

Is God not listening? Or have we misapplied the meaning of "pulling down" strongholds? It's obvious to me that the application of this passage is wrong. The *"strongholds"* Paul was referring to had nothing directly to do with *"spiritual forces of evil in the heavenly realms"* (Ephesians 6:12), but rather with *"arguments and every pretension that sets itself up against the knowledge of God"* (2 Corinthians 10:5).

> *While demons work directly against us, fallen angels use tactics that are more indirect in nature.*

Satan's headquarters may exist in the "heavenly realms," but the battlefield is in our *minds*. You can shout at the forces in heaven until your voice grows hoarse, but if you are not doing your part to change the thinking of your community, you have lost your voice for nothing. Worse, your community will remain under the influence of the kingdom of darkness.

To understand more clearly our strategy for spiritual warfare against fallen angels, we must first recognize these beings. While demons work *directly* against us, fallen angels use tactics that are more *indirect* in nature. It is easy to recognize a demonic attack and what must be done in response—rebuke it and command it to go. But what do you do when a spiritual force in the heavenlies attacks?

Although in God's eyes we are *"raised...up with Christ and seated...with him in the heavenly realms"* (Ephesians 2:6), our temporary residence remains in this world. Because we are seated with Him in heavenly places, we have authority in this realm, but how we exercise that authority over fallen angels is different from the way we exercise our authority over demons. Once again, I come back to this point: a ground soldier fights the enemy on the ground by using certain weapons, but he uses different and more powerful ones on enemy aircraft. The same is true of fallen angels. We can confront them directly through commands of faith; however, we need to employ additional and more powerful weapons, as well.

In the next chapter, I will describe seven powerful weapons we can use to defeat the forces of these angels.

Chapter Ten

How to Deal with Fallen Angels

The conclusion I have reached concerning how to deal with fallen angels has taken much time, thought, prayer, and Bible study. This, combined with years of experience, has led me to these seven ways of dealing with fallen angels, which, if practiced, will hinder, limit, and even defeat their power and influence in this world.

1. Cast Out Demons

Demons are Satan's first line of defense. In order to make any progress against the heavenly forces, you must penetrate their strongholds. If a particular area has a large number of demons, you have no choice but to deal with them directly.

The occult is a form of false religion in which people tap into spiritual forces for power, such as voodoo, witchcraft, psychic readings, or New Age practices. In places where these practices are prevalent, I have encountered large numbers of demonized people. Some of the most unusual deliverance services I have ever seen have been in areas dominated by the occult.

During the first night of a particular service in Africa, I gave a call for people to be healed. A man came forward and was healed by the Lord. Soon afterward, however, he began

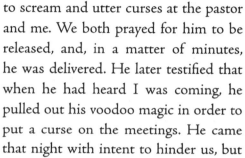

Fallen angels are hurt when we cast out demons.

to scream and utter curses at the pastor and me. We both prayed for him to be released, and, in a matter of minutes, he was delivered. He later testified that when he had heard I was coming, he pulled out his voodoo magic in order to put a curse on the meetings. He came that night with intent to hinder us, but he found that he was kept from disrupting our meeting by the power of God. Enthralled by the message, he came forward, and, to his surprise, was healed. At that point, the evil spirits within him reacted violently before being driven out for good.

These cases are common in countries where the occult is practiced openly. I am concerned for highly developed nations that are experiencing an increased fascination with the occult. There seem to be more and more movies and TV programs dealing with themes of the occult, as well.

I believe that fallen angels are hurt when we cast out demons, primarily because of Jesus' response to His followers when they returned from a mission trip. They said to the Lord, *"Even the demons submit to us in your name"* (Luke 10:17). Notice His response to their wonderful testimonies of exorcisms:

> *I saw Satan fall like lightning from heaven. I have given you authority to trample on snakes and*

scorpions and to overcome all the power of the enemy; nothing will harm you. (Luke 10:18–19)

Satan, it seems, lost ground in the heavenly realms that day. Some believe this is merely a reference to Satan's original fall from heaven. Perhaps that is true, but what a strange context in which to interject such information. I believe Jesus was also referring to what was presently happening to Satan because of the success His disciples had in driving out demons. In other words, by defeating Satan's demons, we are also administering personal defeats to the devil.

2. Intercessory Prayer

Intercessory prayer is very much a lost art. Many Christians will race through the Lord's Prayer or throw out a quick prayer for blessing or protection, but they know little of agonizing, intense, wrestling prayer in the spirit. Intercessory prayer is often associated with fasting. Unfortunately, most believers do not want to experience the sacrifice of the flesh involved in fasting. It seems difficult and unnecessary. Yet prayer and fasting must often be combined if we are to see results.

Daniel's example is a good case study. Weary of experiencing the ongoing captivity of his people, Daniel came across the prophecy of Jeremiah that predicted their captivity but also gave the time frame for when God's people would be liberated. Daniel discovered that the time was now!

In anticipation of this prophetic promise, Daniel began to seek the Lord in prayer.

> *At that time I, Daniel, mourned for three weeks. I ate no choice food; no meat or wine touched my lips; and I used no lotions at all until the three weeks were over.* (Daniel 10:2–3)

Intercessory prayer is a time of mourning and of grieving over a loss. You haven't really interceded for the lost if you have not experienced mourning for their souls. You must feel their pain, their distress, and their lost condition. Often, you will even weep for them in prayer, longing for them to come to salvation.

Unfortunately, we are often so caught up in our own problems that we do not have time to be concerned for others.

You haven't interceded for the lost if you have not mourned for their souls. You must feel their pain, their distress, and their lost condition.

If the minister calls on members to come to the church for a time of intercessory prayer, few will likely show up unless they have a personal motivation to come. How are we to remove the forces of evil when we are so bound by them? It's time to shake off our selfishness and our weak flesh and pray for the lost.

Daniel continued, "*I was standing on the bank of the great river, the Tigris*" (verse 4). He was not in his prayer closet, but at a place of commerce, a place where major deals took place. Intercessory prayer must be practiced with an expectation of great change. Daniel went to a place to where changes in the political landscape would take place. He had faith that his prayer would be answered.

It's not a bad idea to pray and then go to the places where laws are made, ideas are propagated, or commerce is done. Demonstrate to God that you believe He will make a change. It was there at the Tigris River that Daniel was told about the future of the world and of Israel. This revelation was intended to show the future Israelites how to plan for the future, what political regimes they were to support, and, more importantly, the time when their Messiah would come.

Paul described this type of intercessory prayer by comparing the process to childbirth: *"I am again in the pains of childbirth until Christ is formed in you"* (Galatians 4:19). Giving birth is painful and takes much energy. Intercessory prayer is like that.

Epaphras was a great role model for this type of prayer. About him, Paul wrote, *"He is always wrestling in prayer for you, that you may stand firm in all the will of God, mature and fully assured"* (Colossians 4:12). It is not easy to wrestle, but Epaphras knew he was in a spiritual battle for the well-being of the church. The word *wrestle* is taken from the word for *agonize*. The idea is that you agonize and suffer over your community. You are not satisfied with how they are living. You know that God has something better for them, and you pray until it happens.

You become like Nehemiah, who, when he heard that the walls of Jerusalem were in disrepair, said, *"When I heard these things, I sat down and wept. For some days I mourned and fasted and prayed before the God of heaven"* (Nehemiah 1:4). He then identified with the sins of the people: *"I confess the* sins we Israelites, including myself and my father's house, have committed against you" (verse 6). Too many condescending saints pray for people but, deep in their hearts, have no understanding of their pain and how they have contributed to it.

As long as we are judging people instead of identifying with them, we will never enter the heart of God, touch heaven, or push back the forces of darkness.

3. Preach the Gospel

> *I am not ashamed of the gospel, because it is the power of God for the salvation of everyone who believes.* (Romans 1:16)

Satan's currency is souls. The more souls he has, the greater influence he has over the world. Satan's greatest fear is to see a soul saved. When a person hears and begins to understand the gospel, his eyes are opened and he turns from darkness to light. As he does so, he leaves Satan's domain; thus, Satan loses influence.

Satan's currency is souls. The more souls he has, the greater influence he has over the world.

To Satan, people are nothing more than a commodity. He uses them for his purposes. When a person is saved and leaves his dominion, Satan loses some effectiveness and cannot supply his fallen angels with needed ammunition to continue poisoning the environment.

Early in my ministry, I was invited to speak at a large and famous ballroom in El Paso called the Sancho Brothers'

Ballroom. It was known for parties, drunkenness, and all sorts of evil. I arrived and presented the gospel, and many people responded by accepting salvation. Among the people who were eventually saved were the four brothers who owned the ballroom. Their business closed soon after as they went into Christian vocations. Because of their conversion, it became less likely for people to get drunk and fall into sexual sin. Satan needs souls to wage his war against creation. It is no wonder that he will do his best to persecute an anointed preacher of the gospel. Satan will do anything in his power to keep people from listening to God's word. Thus, an important way we wage war against fallen angels is by preaching the gospel so that others will be converted.

4. Utilize the Media

The origin of the word *Hollywood* actually comes from "Holy Wood." Perhaps the town had a calling from God to inspire the world with its movies—stir them with stories of redemption, of good winning over evil, and of lifting the human spirit so people will aspire to be better. Somewhere along the race for the almighty dollar, Hollywood obviously lost its bearings. It never became anchored in the Holy Wood—the cross—or in the blood of Christ. Without the meaning of the cross, Hollywood seems to put out only the kind of trash that debases human beings. Sex sells, so they enthusiastically produce what people want to buy.

As believers, we know that profit should not get in the way of being prophetic. Of course sin sells; no one argues the point. The issue is about what will motivate us: the "love of money" or the "love of people"? After all, people want drugs, too, but that doesn't mean we should open shops for drug dealers just because there is a need.

Don't wait for the executives in Hollywood to have a change of heart. It's time for believers to win back Hollywood—not just the movies, but all forms of mass communication. Preaching the gospel is about communication. There is so much more to communication than standing behind a pulpit and delivering a sermon.

Mass media encompasses all the various forms of disseminating information. It includes the printed forms of newspapers, magazines, and books. It also includes radio, television, film, and the Internet. Mass media can produce lectures, news, documentaries, and advertisements, as well as entertainment through stories and music. Believers are not called to abandon any form of mass media. On the contrary, we are called to *"Go into all the world and preach the good news to all creation"* (Mark 16:15).

We must go beyond mere "talking head" lectures if we are going to compete with the world for the eyes and ears of "all creation."

We must go beyond mere "talking head" lectures if we are going to compete with the world for the eyes and ears of *"all creation."* We must publish the good news in all forms. I believe God is raising up movie producers and directors who will once again inspire audiences with stories that speak of redemption and morality. God is calling news reporters who will tell stories that challenge people to a nobler life. God is calling Internet-savvy believers to creatively share the gospel in cyberspace. God is speaking to authors who will write books and scripts that will touch the heart of hurting humanity. There are songwriters who will compose the tunes and lyrics they hear from heaven.

My son, Justin, and three other friends from Baylor University were talking with another friend who had attempted suicide. They tried encouraging him to get his mind off his problems and do something adventurous. *Like what?* he wondered.

They gave several suggestions, but one in particular stood out: why not ride their bikes from Waco, Texas, to Anchorage, Alaska? After mulling this over and discussing it, they suddenly turned to each other and said, in unison, "Hey, what's keeping us from doing this? Let's do it!"

They logged on to the social networking Internet site *Facebook* and made a challenge: if 250,000 people would join their *Facebook* group, the four guys would take the challenge and ride their bikes from Texas to Alaska. They figured they would never get that many people to support them. Imagine their surprise when their challenge was met within eleven days!

Since then, they have launched a new Internet site with all the "bells and whistles" that attract young viewers. They have been the subject of features by several newspapers and television stations and have captured the attention of the secular world. MTV has worked with them to air their favorite songs on their online site. Between the songs, they talk about suicide prevention and give little snippets of inspiration without becoming too preachy. These guys are doing the kinds of things that I believe God wants all of us to do—use all available means of technology and media to reach people with the good news of the gospel.

Instead of abandoning the airways, we need to take on Satan—*"the ruler of the kingdom of the air"* (Ephesians 2:2)—and show him who really owns the air! We are truly engaging and defeating the demonic forces when we use the mass media for the glory of God.

5. Influence the Schools

Jay is a very experienced history teacher. Despite his success in the school system, he once came to me and expressed his frustration with his vocation.

"Pastor, I feel like I am doing nothing when I know there is a world that needs to be set free." He explained how impressed he was with my work. He, too, wanted to travel and hold miracle, deliverance, and healing meetings around the world. Despite all his efforts, however, he had not received any invitations to preach. "What am I supposed to do with my life?" he asked.

Jay, like many Spirit-filled believers, had a limited understanding of spiritual warfare. He confined it to revival meetings where a minister would drive out demons and engage the congregation in spiritual warfare prayers. Little did he know that he had an opportunity to engage in spiritual warfare right where God had put him—a school.

I explained to Jay that he, of all people, should know how secular humanists are trying to eradicate any vestige of Christianity from the school system, and that he had a real opportunity to pull down the strongholds in the minds of children by showing them the real history of our nation. He could explain the role of the Bible when it came to the writing of our constitution. He had a chance to show that the founders of our nation were devout Christians and that God was active in the founding of our country. Jay had ample room to help his students understand the spiritual roots of our nation. As I explained this to Jay, he smiled and realized that his vocation was an actual calling from God.

Secular humanists are clever. They know the way to eliminate Christianity from our society is to begin with our children. Children are like clay. When clay is first made, it easy to mold, but as time goes by, it hardens and becomes difficult to shape. Therefore, secular humanists go after children. They try to convince them that God doesn't exist. They promote the teaching of natural evolution at the exclusion of creationism. They twist the words of our founding forefathers and make it appear as though they were secularists. They hand out condoms and lie to our children by telling them that sex is "safe." It may be safer, but it is far from safe. They tell our children that there are no moral laws, and if it feels good, do it—just be "safe" when doing it. They hand out books to preadolescent children such as *Heather Has Two Mommies*. They try to brainwash our children into viewing sinful lifestyles as normal, acceptable behavior.

Unfortunately, they seem to be gaining ground. According to the Barna Group, a 2007 study showed that a group of 16- to 29-year-olds are "more skeptical of and resistant to Christianity" than the same demographic a decade ago. If we fail to turn the tide in the school system, the next generation will have more demonic strongholds that will be increasingly difficult to pull down.

If we fail to turn the tide in the school system, the next generation will have more demonic strongholds that will be difficult to pull down.

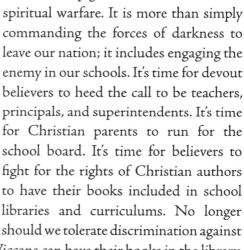

Do not pigeonhole the methods of spiritual warfare. It is more than simply commanding the forces of darkness to leave our nation; it includes engaging the enemy in our schools. It's time for devout believers to heed the call to be teachers, principals, and superintendents. It's time for Christian parents to run for the school board. It's time for believers to fight for the rights of Christian authors to have their books included in school libraries and curriculums. No longer should we tolerate discrimination against Christianity—if Wiccans can have their books in the library, so should Christians.

As a parent, you are engaging in spiritual warfare by getting involved in the PTA and working to see that your children get the kind of honest and moral education they need to become the kind of people God made them to be.

6. Get Involved in Politics

This subject may seem taboo, but it should not be. The terms in Scripture for evil entities are *"rulers," "authorities,"* and *"powers"* (Ephesians 6:12). These words come from governmental terms. Satan, as a matter of fact, was called the King of Tyre (see Ezekiel 28:12) and the prince of Persia (see Daniel 10:20). It's no accident that angels are given political and military terms. Their work is primarily among human leaders who make laws or wage war.

Satan hates it when true believers get involved in the political process to enact just and moral laws in the land. Laws affect the behavior of people. They cannot change hearts, but they can change actions and therefore keep people out of sinful bondages.

Satan hates it when true believers get involved in the political process to enact just and moral laws in the land.

In Holland, for example, the laws are very liberal—including the legalization of some drug use and prostitution. It is no coincidence that it is an uphill battle to penetrate this society with the gospel. The people there are so blinded by sin that it is difficult for them to see the light.

> *This is the verdict: Light has come into the world, but men loved darkness instead of light because their deeds were evil. Everyone who does evil hates the light, and will not come into the light for fear that his deeds will be exposed.* (John 3:19–20)

According to Scripture, the principle is quite clear: the worse people's deeds are, the more difficult it is for them to be saved. In a city or nation that permits much evil behavior, the people's hearts become hardened toward the gospel.

> *They are darkened in their understanding and separated from the life of God because of the ignorance that is in them due to the hardening of their hearts. Having lost all sensitivity, they have*

> *given themselves over to sensuality so as to indulge*
> *in every kind of impurity, with a continual lust for*
> *more.* (Ephesians 4:18–19)

When sinful practices are readily available, permitted, and even applauded, people become bound by them, and the only thing they desire is more of them.

The gospel calls people to repent from sin, but because of the need for repentance, many are unwilling to become Christians because they love their sin more than God. It is hard to reach a city that is so entrenched in immorality. They *"loved darkness instead of light."* Why? Because *"their deeds were evil."*

A government's responsibility is outlined clearly in Romans 13:4: *"The authorities are established by God for that very purpose, to punish those who do wrong"* (NLT). Government goes astray when it ignores this call. It becomes an instrument of the devil when it punishes the good and rewards the bad. This includes, but is not limited to, laws regarding abortion rights, same-sex marriages, zoning laws favoring sex clubs, and restrictions on the free and public expression of religion. Even school boards have control over textbooks, curriculums, sexual education, and other information that is presented to impressionable students.

When Christians prayerfully enter the realm of politics and government, either through voting, campaigning, financing, or running for office, the fallen angels and demons tremble. They recognize the importance of lawmaking and policy shaping in influencing how people react to the gospel.

Consider how difficult it is to penetrate the Middle East with the gospel—the laws there forbid conversion to Christianity. The conversion rate there is nearly zero because civil punishments make people afraid to become Christians.

To break the power of the evil hosts in heaven, Christians need to become involved in civic and political affairs.

7. Obey God

And we will be ready to punish every act of disobedience, once your obedience is complete.

(2 Corinthians 10:6)

This passage speaks about spiritual warfare and taking captive every thought. Paul reminded the church at Corinth of the spiritual law of responsibility and authority: the more responsible you are, the more authority you will be given.

We must not fool ourselves into thinking that we can change the world if we cannot even change ourselves. Paul made it clear: once your obedience is complete, *then* you will be ready to punish every act of disobedience. We will have the spiritual authority to push back the forces of darkness when we obey God.

Paul wrote to his friend, Timothy, giving him good counsel about whom to ordain as pastors: *"He must also have a good reputation with outsiders, so that he will not fall into disgrace and into the devil's trap"* (1 Timothy 3:7). Satan sets traps, especially for spiritual leaders. If he can get them to fall, then he can bring disgrace upon them. As a result, they will lose their credibility and it will be hard for them

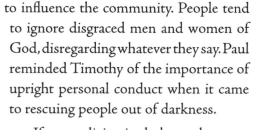

We must not fool ourselves into thinking that we can change the world if we cannot change ourselves.

to influence the community. People tend to ignore disgraced men and women of God, disregarding whatever they say. Paul reminded Timothy of the importance of upright personal conduct when it came to rescuing people out of darkness.

If we are living in darkness, how can we rescue anybody? When a general in God's army falls, the fallen angels have more ammunition with which to spread their lies and it becomes increasingly difficult to persuade the unsaved of their need for salvation because of the hypocrisy they see in the church. "*God's name is blasphemed among the Gentiles because of you*" (Romans 2:24).

Often, the worst part of a minister falling is not the sin itself, but the response of the body of Christ. In many cases, the world does not see our love and forgiveness on display, but our scorn and vindictiveness are usually obvious.

Many years ago, when the sexual sin of Jim Bakker and Jessica Hahn came to light, what most of the world witnessed was how other ministers dealt with him. "He is a cancer that needs to be excised," one minister said. Others were quick to mock and ridicule a weak and injured brother. Some ministers even jockeyed about in an attempt to inherit Bakker's lucrative PTL television network.

I believe that painful incident set the body of Christ back for many years. Yes, the sin was first that of Jim Bakker. If he had not fallen into temptation, there would have been no room for the devil to bring his accusations. The sin, pride, and cruelty that followed, however, gave the fallen angels much material with which to work.

On the other hand, when we stand with integrity while others are caving in, we have an opportunity to change the way the world views us as Christians.

Once again, consider Daniel. He was tested by an unfair, immoral law that said that if he did not quit praying to God, he would be thrown into the lions' den. Nevertheless, Daniel defied the law and continued his prayer routine with God. He received his punishment and was tossed into the lions' lair, but God

When we stand with integrity while others are caving in, we have an opportunity to change the way the world views Christians.

protected him, and he came out without a scratch.

King Darius was so overjoyed that he issued this decree:

> *In every part of my kingdom people must fear and reverence the God of Daniel. For he is the living God and he endures forever; his kingdom will not be destroyed, his dominion will never end.*
>
> (Daniel 6:26)

This incident provided a great opportunity for evangelism. People had a chance to examine the claim of Judaism—that there is only one God—all because one man stood with integrity and lived the way God intended. No evil spiritual principality could stop it.

We can shout at the forces of evil in heavenly places all day long. We can command them to come down. We can rebuke them and tell them to leave our cities, but it is our simple acts of obedience that will really inflict damage on the forces of Satan.

Chapter Eleven

The Battleground of the Mind

Have you ever desired to break a bad habit, only to feel as though you didn't have the willpower to gain victory? As hard as you tried, sin kept dragging you down with deep feelings of guilt and shame. There are times when you feel you are making real progress in your walk with God, then—*bam!*—a situation comes up that leaves you powerless, and the oppression seems to grip you all over again. You thought things would change once you were saved, yet your life remains a losing struggle. Even though you know in your mind that you are new creation, in your heart you feel like the same old person you used to be. Then, you heard about spiritual deliverance and decided to give that a try. It worked! At first, you felt free—the heavy burden was lifted—but slowly, your nasty little secret came right back again.

What's the real problem?

Were you ever really delivered?

Did all the demons really leave?

The answer is quite simple: your mind is the battleground and target of Satan's assaults, and, unfortunately, you never learned how to fight this battle.

This was the problem for the Israelites when they exited Egypt. *"It takes eleven days to go from Horeb to Kadesh Barnea by the Mount Seir road"* (Deuteronomy 1:2). Think about it: an eleven-day trip led to a forty-year odyssey. They became lost, not because they did not have a clear map—God's Word provided all the directions they needed—but because they failed to *follow* the map.

Satan works on the minds of saints just as he does sinners.

I don't doubt that some of you reading this book should be further along in your Christian walk by now, but instead you are continuing to cling to old thought patterns and sinful ways. You still struggle with the same old sins, the same old sickness, and the same old problems.

We have already discovered that, prior to being saved, your mind was blinded by the devil.

> *The god of this age has blinded the minds of unbelievers, so that they cannot see the light of the gospel of the glory of Christ, who is the image of God.* (2 Corinthians 4:4)

Do not think, however, that because the devil failed to keep you from being saved, that he will relinquish the fight for your mind. Satan works on the minds of saints just as he does with sinners.

For though we live in the world, we do not wage war as the world does. The weapons we fight with are not the weapons of the world. On the contrary, they have divine power to demolish strongholds. We demolish arguments and every pretension that sets itself up against the knowledge of God, and we take captive every thought to make it obedient to Christ.   (2 Corinthians 10:3–5)

Our spiritual combat zone is in the mind, where we must take every thought captive. Many will lay their problems at the feet of psychics or witch doctors, saying, "He put a spell on me, and this is my problem." Wrong! Your mind, which feared the curse, is the problem—not the curse itself. Some hyperdeliverance believers think their problems exist because not all of their demons were cast out of them during their last deliverance session. Wrong again! In truth, such believers have never been established in the knowledge of their own spiritual authority. They have never acted as children of God but rather as babes in Christ, looking for others to win the victory that Christ has already won.

The arena in which you will fight Satan is not Madison Square Garden or the Coliseum; it is the "thought dome"— the place where all reasoning, ideas, opinions, and beliefs either win or lose. True belief in God will create the lasting victory you desire. False or twisted beliefs create a losing environment that will only keep you in bondage.

Two Creations

"For as he thinketh within himself, so is he" (Proverbs 23:7 ASV). You are the sum total of your thoughts. Your life is the result of the thoughts going on within you. My thoughts about you do not make you who you are; only your thoughts create the kind of person you are.

A man's hatred of me will never destroy me. My hatred of myself, however, will sink me. Another person's prejudice against me will never keep me from success, but my own self-rejection will hamper me from prosperity. In the same way, Satan's view of me cannot defeat me unless I adopt his outlook.

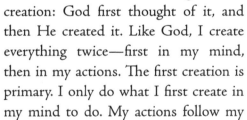

Satan's view of me cannot defeat me unless I adopt his outlook.

I discovered something about creation: God first thought of it, and then He created it. Like God, I create everything twice—first in my mind, then in my actions. The first creation is primary. I only do what I first create in my mind to do. My actions follow my thoughts. This is why Peter said, *"Prepare your minds for action"* (1 Peter 1:13). Preparation is really like an army boot camp where you nourish your mind by feeding it the right diet of faith, hope, and love, and you exercise it by acting on the Word.

1. Your Thoughts Influence Your Relationships

"People don't like me."

If this statement is true for you, the reason is most likely the way you think. You think poorly of yourself or others, and you don't realize how those thoughts push people away.

In his book *Favor, The Road to Success*, Bob Buess tells the story of a woman who wrote to tell him how bad everything was in her life. She was attractive but could not get a date with any young men. She had a negative spirit.

Bob wrote back to her, "I don't blame them for not liking you. I'm afraid I could not like you myself." He wrote that in order to shock her. Then, he encouraged her to change her attitude about others and herself. He sent her Scripture passages about favor and told her to confess them about herself each day. It worked. She wrote back later to tell him that she was engaged.

Eventually, Bob actually met the woman and her fiancé— not the same one that she originally became engaged to, but another one. She eventually married the second guy. Once she changed her thoughts, this woman began to improve her relationships.

2. Your Thoughts Create Your Circumstances

"Whatever will be, will be."

That is the victim's mantra.

God never intended for you to be a victim, but a victor. Many Christians feel powerless over their situations. They fail to realize that there is a treasure of wisdom and power within them that they have failed to open.

Vanessa was sexually abused as a child. She was an incredibly beautiful woman, but she was insecure about herself. She went through many plastic surgeries to transform her body into what she thought men wanted—including large breast implants. This sense of insecurity led her to men who tended to abuse her. She expected trash; she got trash.

Fortunately, through the invitation of a friend, Vanessa started to attend a church that believed in a good God. She realized that she had "subconsciously" believed that God was like the men in her life—angry and demeaning. She came to the realization that God loved her and wanted her to have a better life. No longer would she tolerate abusive men. She had her implants removed and learned to appreciate the way God had made her. Today, she is a successful businesswoman who stands on her own two feet and in the power of God.

3. Your Thoughts Produce Health and Finances

"Divine health is good, if God wants me to have it."

This may be a humble statement, but it is not an expression of confident, bold—or even biblical—faith. Bold faith is like that of the Canaanite woman who would not give up until Christ released her. In the eyes of most, she should have given up after the disciples turned her away, but she persisted. Jesus tested the woman, calling her a dog. Undeterred, she reminded Him that even dogs were able to eat the crumbs from beneath the table. Jesus answered, *"'Woman, you have great faith! Your request is granted.' And her daughter was healed from that very hour"* (Matthew 15:28). It is easy to feel sorry for yourself when you are in pain, but feeling sorry for yourself will never create faith.

A good friend of mine, John, is a successful businessman and minister, but if you knew how he grew up, you would never think that he could have become as rich as he is. He grew up in the poorest part of El Paso, Texas. Raised by a single mom in an apartment building that inspectors nearly shut down for rat infestation, John thought that poverty was his lot in life.

It is easy to feel sorry for yourself when you are in pain, but feeling sorry for yourself will never create faith.

Eventually, he was saved and began attending a Spirit-filled church, but his pastor did not believe much in God's people having the right to prosper. The church reflected the philosophy of its

pastor and struggled constantly with money. It wasn't until John moved to Phoenix, Arizona, that he discovered that God had a plan to prosper him. The pastor taught about the biblical steps to financial freedom, and John soaked up the message. Today, he is a successful businessman and author who helps others find their ways into abundance. John says that the key is your thought life. Think abundance, and abundance will come to you.

4. Your Thoughts Form Your Character

"It won't hurt to look at this magazine; I'm only looking, not touching."

Those are usually the last thoughts a person has before falling into temptation and sin. Compromise in the small things often leads to compromise in the big things. Thoughts are the seeds of action. Action is the seed of habit. Habit is the seed of one's lifestyle. Lifestyle is the seed of one's life.

Darlene has been through several relationships in the past few years, and, to this day, she blames the men for the breakups. It has never dawned on her that she might be part of the problem. When you witness Darlene's personality, however, it becomes evident that she has some real issues.

When she was young, Darlene attended a conservative church, but she rebelled against the idea of being obedient to God; instead, she embraced the idea that she was free to do what she wanted. By the age of fourteen, she was sexually active, and she never slowed down, jumping from one empty relationship to another. Most of the time, she was looking for a "sugar daddy" who would provide for her financially, and she occasionally suckered a few men into doing it. When she wasn't being provided for, she found some work—never meaningful and always short-term. She tried college but dropped out soon after enrolling.

Darlene admits that she sometimes wants to end it all. Because Darlene is in the darkness, she cannot see the light. Her constant thoughts of rebellion have created her present unpleasant reality—an extremely unhappy and unfulfilling life.

In order to make a positive, lasting change in your life, you are going to have to change the way you think and win the battle for your mind.

Chapter Twelve

Seven Ways Christians Give Ground to Satan

In sports, the home field advantage is a huge benefit. Traveling to the opposing team's home field makes victory harder to achieve. The same is true for your mind. There are several different mind-sets that create a home field advantage for Satan. I will list seven mind-sets that put the believer at a disadvantage.

1. The Unconverted Mind

Believe it or not, it's possible to be saved without your mind having been truly converted. Salvation is called being "born again." Jesus taught that it is your "spirit" that is renewed, not your body and mind.

> No one can enter the kingdom of God unless he is born of water and the Spirit. Flesh gives birth to flesh, but the Spirit gives birth to spirit. You should not be surprised at my saying, "You must be born again." (John 3:5–7)

The born-again experience is not necessarily an emotional or physical experience; it is primarily a spiritual experience. It is the rebirth of the human spirit. "*He saved us through the washing of rebirth and renewal by the Holy Spirit"* (Titus 3:5). The Holy Spirit gives birth only to spirit, not flesh.

In order to receive the new birth, you have to repent. The Greek word for this is *metanoeo*, which means "to change your thinking." You cannot be converted without changing the way you think about the basic claims of Jesus Christ. Once you accept Him and make Him your Lord, you are saved. However, you are not required to completely change your mind in that moment in order to be saved. Just enough change of mind is all that is needed to be saved.

The Holy Spirit gives birth only to spirit, not flesh.

When you were saved, Satan failed to keep you from seeing the *"light of the gospel of the glory of Christ"* (2 Corinthians 4:4), yet he often succeeds at keeping you from seeing the light of the gospel of the *teachings* of Christ. It's possible to not totally understand or even accept all the teachings of Christ through the gospels, epistles, and the illumination of the Spirit concerning the Old Testament Scriptures.

It is an ignorance of Scripture or a refusal to submit to Scripture that gives Satan the opportunity to stop the fruit of your salvation. He was unsuccessful at keeping the root from being planted, but he often excels at keeping the tree from growing fruit.

The only way to experience victory in the mind is to renew it as you renewed your spirit. *"Do not conform any longer to the pattern of this world, but be transformed by the renewing of your mind"* (Romans 12:2). Satan, the god of this world, desires your lifestyle to mimic the world; the only way he is defeated is by the believer renewing his mind with the wisdom of Christ. As long as the believer continues with the same philosophies, ideologies, moral values, and anti-supernatural biases of the world, he will continue to struggle in his mind. The mind that thinks wrongly will cause a person to act wrongly.

2. The Polluted Mind

A believer may know the thoughts he should think, but often what he knows is not what he does—as the old saying goes, "Garbage in, garbage out." If you keep feeding your mind junk, it will continue to produce junk. You cannot feed your mind filth and expect a clean life. It doesn't work that way.

Satan loves for believers to read and watch junk. No amount of deliverance will help you if you continue to look at evil things. We need to make a covenant similar to Job's: *"I made a covenant with my eyes not to look lustfully at a girl"* (Job 31:1). A covenant is sealed in blood. This speaks of sacrifice.

> *You cannot feed your mind filth and expect a clean life. It doesn't work that way.*

It is a sacrifice to avoid looking lustfully at a beautiful woman or a handsome man. It is not possible to avoid noticing beauty, but this passage is not about avoiding beauty—it's about avoiding *lust*. Lustful thoughts are a fertile breeding ground for evil spirits.

3. The Doubtful Mind

> *He who doubts is like a wave of the sea, blown and tossed by the wind. That man should not think he will receive anything from the Lord; he is a double-minded man, unstable in all he does.*

(James 1:6–8)

The Lord does not appreciate it when His children do not believe Him. When God tells us to do something or to trust in something and we disobey, we open the door for the devil to continue bombarding our thoughts with confusion.

One ministry partner of mine kept sending donations to our ministry, then wrote to us saying he didn't agree with our teachings. Then he wrote again and sent money, apologizing for the previous letter. Then he wrote yet again, saying he made a mistake in giving us money because he didn't believe in what we preached. This is a person the devil loves; he is *"unstable in all he does."*

He listened to the Word of God and then to unfruitful theological arguments, which confused him as to the truthfulness of the gifts of the Spirit—tongues, healing, miracles, and prophecy. This believer needs to close his ears to ministers who do not have a supernatural ministry. I don't want to be sectarian, but I believe that a supernatural ministry—one with signs and wonders—bears proof of the Holy Spirit's endorsement. Many believers, however, like the one I mentioned, are too easily swayed by every so-called Bible teacher when many of these teachers do not have ministries of miracles.

Part of the armor we are called to put on is the shield of faith (see Ephesians 6:16); however, if our faith is weak, we are subject to the onslaughts of the devil. Be sure that, in your mind, you believe the clear Word of God.

4. The Heretical Mind

There will always be minor differences of interpretation of various passages of Scripture; however, there is a clear demarcation between respectful disagreements and heretical doctrine.

> *But there were also false prophets among the people, just as there will be false teachers among you. They will secretly introduce destructive heresies, even denying the sovereign Lord who bought them—bringing swift destruction on themselves.*
>
> (2 Peter 2:1)

Heresy is *destructive*. The word *destroy* means "to ruin, including physical, spiritual, or eternal loss." Any teaching that ruins people's lives, or causes them to lose their physical lives, their spiritual walks with God, or their own salvation, is heresy.

Heresy usually begins with a dominant leader who feels he is someone special. To disagree with this person is to disagree with God. He is an overlord of the flock, not a shepherd. He starts by isolating the disciples from the rest of the universal church. He is able to introduce further heretical teachings because the followers are so isolated.

It is no wonder that such a group eventually becomes a cult. Cult members are easy targets for Satan's assaults. He

If you were ever involved in a cult, it is important for you to renounce the leader and all of his teachings.

works further on their minds, convincing them to do unchristian things such as storing up weapons, leaving the cities, or breaking off all communication with relatives and friends. This behavior can lead people to harm themselves. I have seen this scenario played out in America and around the world among cults that commit mass suicides.

A person who has left a cult will need to reject each and every false teaching he ever accepted. I have had difficulties with some ex-cult members because they still hold on, possibly for emotional security, to some of their former teachings and practices. If you were ever involved in a cult, no matter how harmless you believe it was, it is important for you to renounce the leader and all of his teachings. It is important that you begin afresh with the gospel.

5. The Naïve Mind

Dear friends, do not believe every spirit, but test the spirits to see whether they are from God, because many false prophets have gone out into the world.
(1 John 4:1)

Some Christians are just plain gullible. When someone appears spiritual, puts on a mystical act, and pretends he is listening to God, some innocent Christians begin to believe him.

I heard the story of an evangelist who clandestinely placed feathers on people while she preached. Then, someone screamed out, "My God, the Holy Spirit is here! Here is one of His feathers!" Sadly, some believers encouraged others to attend the meetings because of this so-called miracle.

Another area of naïveté is when "exorcists" control their subjects by convincing them that there are still demons that need to be driven out of them—hopefully over many additional deliverance sessions. I have spoken to many sincere saints who have been in bondage by these frauds. They have usually been through many deliverance sessions, and they come to ask me when they will finally be delivered.

These bondage-makers and their clients were described by the apostle Paul in his second letter to Timothy:

> *They are the kind who worm their way into homes and gain control over weak-willed women, who are loaded down with sins and are swayed by all kinds of evil desires, always learning but never able to acknowledge the truth.* (2 Timothy 3:6–7)

It's not just women who are swayed by these "worms," but men, too. Paul called them *"weak-willed."* This means that they put more confidence in other people's abilities to know God than their own. God does not want you to put complete trust in anyone but Him.

6. The Passive Mind

Some Christians have strange views about hearing from God. They actually believe the way one hears from God is to clear the mind and wait for some external force to activate his thoughts. This is not the biblical way to hear from God.

We are called to think constantly on the Word of God, as Paul said in Philippians:

> *Finally, brothers, whatever is true, whatever is noble, whatever is right, whatever is pure, whatever is lovely, whatever is admirable—if anything is excellent or praiseworthy—think about such things. Whatever you have learned or received or heard from me, or seen in me—put it into practice. And the God of peace will be with you.*
>
> (Philippians 4:8–9)

God's voice sounds like peace—a peace that comes after thinking deeply about spiritual matters, not a peace brought about by the emptying of our minds. Some of the greatest messages God has spoken to me came after I thought deeply about something.

God's voice sounds like peace—a peace that comes after thinking deeply about spiritual matters, not a peace brought about by the emptying of our minds.

I have also noticed that those who struggle to win the battle for their minds often seem to have weak minds. We know that the body becomes strong through exercise and by feeding on the right food. In a similar way, the spirit becomes strong by feeding on a good spiritual diet and by exercising the Word. Just as the body and spirit can become strong, the mind also can become strong through exercise. The stronger your mind is, the less likely it is that the enemy will win.

There are three basic mental exercises I suggest for strengthening the mind.

Concentrate

It is amazing how many people simply do not pay attention to others who are talking to them. Most *pretend* to listen to the other person talk, but they are really thinking about what they are going to say next. When listening to sermons or the reading of Scripture, you need to learn to concentrate.

Read

God chose books as the first means to officially record His Word. He did not wait until we had audio or video recorders; instead, He spoke during a time when people could only write down what He said. I believe television shows and movies have weakened the human mind. It does not take much effort to watch something amusing. It is an easy exercise. The more demanding mental exercise is reading. I have noticed that people who read a lot seem to have fewer problems with their minds than people who opt for passive, mind-numbing entertainment on television.

Memorize

God constantly encourages us to *remember*. It's amazing how we have become so dependent on technology that we don't have to remember things. Our telephones have the option of speed dialing. Our mobile phones pull up names from a directory and call them directly. We don't even know our contacts' numbers anymore. We use calculators to do the simplest math equations. We get books on tape instead of reading the words on the page. In the end, I fear that our minds are becoming weak because of so-called conveniences.

7. The Natural Mind

> *Now the natural man receiveth not the things of the Spirit of God: for they are foolishness unto him; and he cannot know them, because they are spiritually judged.* (1 Corinthians 2:14 ASV)

The *"natural man"* (or person) does not accept the things of the Spirit because he cannot see them. He or she believes only what he can see, touch, hear, smell, and taste. His faith is therefore limited to the five senses.

There is very little in Christianity that is "natural"; most everything is "supernatural."

There are many Christians who resemble the *"natural man"* and struggle with the supernatural. When you get down to it, though, Christianity is a miraculous religion. The prophets predicted Christ's coming; Jesus was born of a virgin; He performed miracles; His sacrifice was a miracle because our sins—which we cannot see—were laid on Him; He was resurrected and ascended into heaven in body, spirit, and soul. Then, to top it all off, the Holy Spirit empowered His disciples to preach supernaturally and to perform miracles. There is very little in Christianity that is "natural"; most everything is "supernatural."

Yet, a large segment of the body of Christ wants to deny the supernatural elements of the faith. This is exactly what Satan wants. He is a supernatural being who works supernaturally to deceive and control people. The only thing that can stop him is the supernatural power of God. The churches and nations that are experiencing the greatest revivals are those moving in the supernatural power of God.

The devil delights in man-made traditions that deny the gifts of the Spirit. One of the casualties to this devilish, cessationist doctrine is the power of deliverance. Satan delights in a church that doesn't believe or participate in casting out demons. Such limited doctrine protects demons from the power of God. Do not buy into a church doctrine that denies any of the spiritual gifts.

Chapter Thirteen

Why Godly People Fall

It is a cardinal mistake to underestimate your opponent. As we should know by now, Satan is quite clever. He doesn't just work on ungodly, irreligious people, but also on believers who are sincere and have a strong devotion to Christ.

There is a misconception that only lukewarm, unholy Christians can be led astray by Satan. When we see a believer fall to lies and temptation, we often assume that he lacks the spiritual knowledge or fervor to overcome the devil's schemes. The apostle Paul saw it differently.

> I am afraid that just as Eve was deceived by the serpent's cunning, your minds may somehow be led astray from your sincere and pure devotion to Christ.　(2 Corinthians 11:3)

Paul was afraid that Satan would hoodwink dedicated believers. Consider how the current landscape of the body of Christ is overflowing with wounded saints—many of whom are strong believers or even full-time ministers at megachurches. This should sound an alarm of Satan's ability to fool even the most loyal of saints.

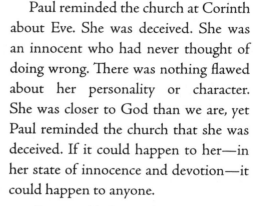

There is a misconception that only lukewarm, unholy Christians can be led astray by Satan.

Paul reminded the church at Corinth about Eve. She was deceived. She was an innocent who had never thought of doing wrong. There was nothing flawed about her personality or character. She was closer to God than we are, yet Paul reminded the church that she was deceived. If it could happen to her—in her state of innocence and devotion—it could happen to anyone.

Scores of believers have fallen prey to Satan. The laundry list of things that trip up Christians is long, and unfortunately not complete:

- Sexual sins (adultery, fornication, pornography, homosexuality, pedophilia)
- Drug and alcohol abuse
- Greed (financial crimes)
- Abuse and control
- Worldliness
- Gambling
- Church strife
- Heresy
- Pride
- Bitterness
- Divorce

I suppose divorce typifies more than any other failure what a shock it is to fall. A couple falls madly in love and say their vows before God. Love is in their eyes. There is not a thought of betrayal in anyone's heart; they are too much in love to suspect that anything could ever go wrong. Lose our love for each other? NEVER!

Nevertheless, couples like the one described often face the tragedy of lost and damaged love. How does it happen? The enemy is subtle and smart.

The same thing can occur in our relationship with God. In the beginning, we are so grateful to God for our salvation. It seems that the more we are forgiven, the more we love. We cannot imagine ever betraying the Lord by our actions, yet some of these same zealous Christians later find themselves trapped beneath layers of ugly, hurtful sin, wondering how they got there.

Since we all are susceptible to frequent sin, Paul warned us not to be overly harsh: *"Brothers, if someone is caught in a sin, you who are spiritual should restore him gently. But watch yourself, or you also may be tempted"* (Galatians 6:1). The "super" saint could easily be offended by such a statement: *"But watch yourself or you also may be tempted."* How could someone who is *spiritual* be capable of falling? He can, if he does not guard his spiritual life carefully.

Paul gave another warning to the saints: *"If you think you are standing firm, be careful that you don't fall!"* (1 Corinthians 10:12). I pose the question, "Do you think you are standing firm?" I hope so, but even if you do, you still must *"be careful that you don't fall."*

Jesus warned the end-time saints, *"Because of the increase of wickedness, the love of most will grow cold"* (Matthew

24:12). Does that shock you? Not just the love of *many*—that would be bad enough—but the love of *most*.

Paul described the final days thusly:

> *There will be terrible times in the last days. People will be lovers of themselves, lovers of money, boastful, proud, abusive, disobedient to their parents, ungrateful, unholy, without love, unforgiving, slanderous, without self-control, brutal, not lovers of the good, treacherous, rash, conceited, lovers of pleasure rather than lovers of God—having a form of godliness but denying its power.*
>
> (2 Timothy 3:1–5)

The word *terrible* should get our attention. It means "dangerous." Some jobs are dangerous. A firefighter who goes into a burning building risks his life. The idea of danger is simple: one mistake could cost you your life. It is one thing for a firefighter to enter the safety of his home and another for him to enter a burning building. Obviously, he must be much more cautious and vigilant when entering the burning building.

We must realize that the world in which we live is like a burning building—the dangers of sin are all around us. We cannot take a lackadaisical approach.

In the past, the world was not nearly as dangerous as it is today. Pornography, which feeds people's lusts and sexual appetites, is freely available at the touch of a button. Divorce, once an act of scorn, is easily obtained, even popular. False religions were not as widespread.

Gambling was isolated in certain states and existed underground, not online and sanctioned by the government. Crime seemed rare and far removed, yet today, for the first time in history, one out of every one hundred Americans is in prison.

Like the firefighter, we must realize that the world in which we live is like a burning building; the dangers of sin are all around us. We cannot take a lackadaisical approach. Over the years, I have counseled many mature believers. Here are some of the tools that Satan used to seduce them.

1. Ambushed by a Sudden Onslaught of Temptation or Trial

"Brothers, if someone is caught in a sin…" (Galatians 6:1). Paul began this verse by describing a believer not as one who willfully and rebelliously turns against God but rather as one who is *"caught in a sin,"* like a hungry bear is caught in a trap. The word for *caught* is the Greek word *prolambano*, meaning "to catch the individual by surprise"—out of the blue, without notice, before he is aware of what is happening.

The King James Version translates the word as "being overtaken." To be overtaken is to be overpowered, like a kidnap victim. In such a case, you don't blame the victim for being kidnapped; it's not his fault. James described the believer as one who *"is tempted when, by his own evil desire, he is dragged away and enticed. Then, after desire has conceived, it gives birth to sin; and sin, when it is full-grown, gives birth to death"* (James 1:14–15). This suggests that the believer is *"dragged away and enticed"* against his will.

It is easy to assume that a fallen believer is someone who "willfully" sinned against God; however, the biblical picture is of one who deeply desires to obey God but is overwhelmed by an onslaught of temptation and trials. It soon becomes more than he can handle, and he falls.

The devil plays on our weakness—a desire for acceptance, a fear of having nothing, a feeling of betrayal—any weak link or vulnerability in our personalities that can be attacked and exploited. No wonder Paul pleaded for the fallen, asking the church to *"restore him gently."* He is already weak and beaten; he doesn't need harsh finger-pointing and accusations of willful disobedience at this point.

The devil plays on any weak link in our personalities that can be attacked and exploited.

Don't misunderstand me. The person who falls is at fault for being caught in sin. The fault, however, is not falling to the temptation as much as it is a failure to *"watch yourself"* (Galatians 6:1). He should have recognized certain weak spots in personality, but instead he put himself in a position to succumb to the temptation.

It is the former addict who begins to hang around old friends, or the middle-aged man who fears growing older and develops a close relationship with a young girl, or the financially troubled woman who desperately tries her luck at gambling. Before they know it, they are popping pills, committing adultery, or bankrupting whatever assets they have left. I've seen it played out many times.

2. Humiliated by Difficult Tests Immediately after an Amazing Spiritual Experience with God

When a believer falls, we usually assume that he was at a low point in his spiritual walk. This, however, is not always true. Consider Elijah. An incredible miracle occurred as a result of his prayers when God sent fire down on his waterlogged sacrifice. (See 1 Kings 18.) This accomplishment brought reformation for Israel and humiliated the prophets of Baal. The people of Israel were ready to listen to Elijah and change their ways. God forgave the nation and sent much-needed rains for their crops.

Elijah was on a spiritual high. Just as his ministry was starting to flourish, however, he received word that Jezebel, the queen, was not happy with him.

> *Jezebel sent a messenger to Elijah to say, "May the gods deal with me, be it ever so severely, if by this time tomorrow I do not make your life like that of one of them."* (1 Kings 19:2)

After all that had happened, Elijah probably should have brushed off Jezebel's threat, but instead, *"Elijah was afraid and ran for his life"* (verse 3). He fell under a tree, and he was not only afraid but guilt-ridden over his lack of courage. *"'I have had enough, LORD,' he said. 'Take my life; I am no better than my ancestors'"* (verse 4).

How could one man fall so deeply into depression and run from his call? Didn't God perform great miracles in response to Elijah's prayers? Didn't the nation of Israel repent? Didn't God send blessings and much-needed rain?

How could Elijah not pass this test after what he had experienced?

Satan will often bring great trials immediately after a great triumph because he knows how dangerous you are to his plans if he leaves you unchecked. Coming on the heels of victory, such trials can often discourage the believer to the point that he succumbs to it. This is what happened with Elijah.

The devil also attempted to do this with Jesus. Jesus had been baptized by John, and the Holy Spirit came upon Him in power. God the Father testified aloud of how pleased He was with His Son. (See Matthew 3:17.) Immediately afterward, however, Jesus was tempted by the devil. (See Matthew 4:1.) Temptation and trial often follow great spiritual milestones with God.

Satan will often bring great trials immediately after a great triumph.

As I look back at my own life, my greatest temptations and trials came after times of great revelation and some of the most powerful experiences I have ever had with God. These tests got to me because, at the time, I felt almost immune to Satan. The tests proved, however, that I was still in a battle—they humbled me.

3. A Bombardment of Mental Suggestions

Satan can supernaturally barrage your mind with the most hideous of thoughts. When this happens, it can make even the most stable Christian question his sanity. Such thoughts do not originate in the heart of the believer. One of the most important revelations you can receive is the fact that not all the thoughts in your mind are really *your* thoughts. Some are actually coming from the voice of Satan.

Do you really think Jesus' own thoughts were to turn stone into bread, leap from the temple, or fall down and worship Satan? (See Matthew 4:3–10.) Of course not! It was the voice of Satan trying to convince Him to do these sinful acts.

While it is true that some thoughts do originate out of a sinful heart, many wicked thoughts actually come from the voice of Satan himself.

Many believers condemn themselves for thinking sinful thoughts. They assume that the ideas originated within their own hearts. While it is true that some thoughts do originate out of a sinful heart, many wicked and abominable thoughts actually come from the voice of Satan himself.

These thoughts, if not recognized and resisted, can take on lives of their own. Soon the believer is dwelling on them. The thoughts start to obsess his mind, and he loses control. The believer grows weak and vulnerable, likely to fall or, worse, to lose his mind.

4. Becoming Isolated

Elijah's failure was actually due to drawing away from people. He thought he was the only one who truly served God. *"I have been very zealous for the LORD God Almighty. The Israelites have rejected your covenant, broken down your altars, and put your prophets to death with the sword. I am the only one left*" (1 Kings 19:14). God confronted him about on his inflated ego, reminding him that there were others who served Him, too: "*I reserve seven thousand in Israel— all whose knees have not bowed down to Baal and all whose mouths have not kissed him*" (verse 18).

Satan will try to woo you away from those people in your life who will identify the seduction and expose the forces of darkness pulling on you. Strategically, Satan tries to keep you away from the people who can help you.

One of the classic symptoms of people falling away from the Lord is seen when they begin to withdraw from their churches, their families, and their friends, until they find themselves alone to battle the forces of darkness. Satan wants you alone. It is at this stage that he can really control you.

When you read or hear stories about mass murderers, what do their neighbors almost always say? "He was a loner. He kept to himself. We didn't see him much. He rarely talked." No wonder demons were able to possess them so completely. No one was there to recognize the problem and prevent it.

5. Determined to Keep the Battle a Private One between You and Satan

> *For the secret power of lawlessness is already at work.* (2 Thessalonians 2:7)

> *It is shameful even to mention what the disobedient do in secret.* (Ephesians 5:12)

Satan works in secret. His victims are convinced they must keep their battles under wraps. They are afraid to let anyone know of the spiritual warfare going on in their souls. Wicked deeds are done in secret. No one advertises his sins. Thus, Satan convinces his prey not to tell anyone else what is going on. Satan fears confession because it releases the soul from his grip.

This is what James was trying to get the fallen Christians to do: *"Confess your sins to each other and pray for each other so that you may be healed"* (James 5:16). There is no healing or deliverance without complete honesty. As long as you keep your deeds secret, they will continue to eat at you. You can tell yourself, *I can beat this on my own.* But you never will. You will always be telling God how sorry you are.

Satan works in secret. His victims are convinced they must keep their battles under wraps.

At first, you feel guilty and lament your failure. Soon, however, you no longer feel any remorse whatsoever. You may still ask God for forgiveness, but you know that you will not be changing your ways any time soon. You are in bondage.

There is only one way to be free: go to a pastor, elder, or leader in the church and confess all the "junk" in your life. He will know how to pray for your spiritual well-being. I have had great success when people have unloaded their sins on me. There is a breakthrough. I see it in their eyes; their tears testify to their real desire to be delivered. After prayer, the demons leave and the joy of salvation returns.

6. So Bewitched, You Feel Overwhelmed and Powerless

"You foolish Galatians! Who has bewitched you?" (Galatians 3:1). There used to be a popular television program called *Bewitched*. It was about a witch named Samantha, who was married to a mortal named Darrin. The plot often revolved around Samantha's mother, Endora, who, in a fit of anger, would sometimes cast spells on Darrin.

In one episode, Endora turned her son-in-law into a donkey. Unable to speak, Darrin could only bray—*heehaw, heehaw, heehaw*. As much as he wanted to act like a man, he could not, because he was *bewitched*.

This is similar to the description Paul gave of what happened to the Galatian church. It summarizes how good people can do bad things and explains how the godly can suddenly become ungodly. It seems a contradiction, but it happens. I have met many wonderful believers who are bewitched. They seem absolutely powerless to overcome the seemingly invisible force that keeps them in bondage. They deeply desire to change, but, as hard as they try, they can't.

I know this feeling all too well. There was a time in my own life when I felt overwhelmed by temptation. I couldn't see a way out of my predicament. People who knew me wondered what had gone wrong. I don't blame them. My mother, knowing of my struggle, pleaded with a local church to pray for me. I knew the church did not particularly like me or believe in everything I taught, but they prayed. On the day they prayed, I was getting a haircut. As the hairstylist was clipping my hair, the blinders on my eyes were removed.

As I sat there in the chair, tears streamed down my cheeks. The hairstylist must have wondered what was going on, but, being a Christian, she remained silent, as she probably knew that God was working on me. In a matter of minutes, I was delivered.

If you are in bondage as you read this, I know what you are feeling. Your eyes are clouded; it is hard to see. You know in your heart what you should do, but your mind is telling you something different. You feel as if a spell is over you. There is a way out! You must pursue honesty and prayer. Go to someone you trust and confess everything—leave nothing out. Ask for prayer and watch what God does.

Chapter Fourteen

Delusional Thoughts

"Hello, this is Pastor Brown, may I help you?" I could hear a little sob coming from the other line.

Finally, a voice cried out, "Pastor Brown, this is Tracy." She began to weep.

"What's wrong, Tracy?"

"I'm dying!"

My heart fell. I thought, *What did the doctor diagnose her with?*

I spoke up, "Tracy, how do you know you're dying?"

"I know because I *feel* it."

My heart calmed down. She had not seen any doctor. She was suffering some sort of panic attack.

The main warning sign that your mind is under satanic attack is a loss of peace. The word *peace* can mean a freedom from hostilities. The opposite of peace is war. When your mind is at war, you live in fear. Peace is the indication that your mind is free from Satan's assaults.

"Thou wilt keep him in perfect peace, whose mind is stayed on thee: because he trusteth in thee" (Isaiah 26:3 KJV). There are

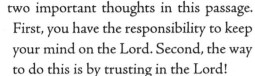

When your mind is at war, you live in fear. Peace is the indication that your mind is free from Satan's assaults.

two important thoughts in this passage. First, you have the responsibility to keep your mind on the Lord. Second, the way to do this is by trusting in the Lord!

Satan will do everything he can to convince you that God is not trustworthy. He will bombard your mind with thoughts of panic. But you can be assured that "*God hath not given us the spirit of fear; but of power, and of love, and of a sound mind*" (2 Timothy 1:7 KJV). A sound mind is your right! Do not settle for anything other than a healthy and whole mind.

Tracy was losing the battle in her mind because she was more convinced of Satan's threats than of God's promises. As I began to minister to her, an insight suddenly entered my heart: many, like Tracy, feel they are losing their minds. The purpose of this chapter is to share the insight God gave me to help Tracy. I hope that it will help you, too, to retain a sound mind.

The Silver Screen of Your Mind

The weapons we fight with are not the weapons of the world. On the contrary, they have divine power to demolish strongholds. We demolish arguments and every pretension that sets itself up against the knowledge of God, and we take captive every thought to make it obedient to Christ.

(2 Corinthians 10:4–5)

I had read this passage many times before, but on one occasion, something new came to me. The word *pretension* struck me. We are told to demolish every pretension. One element of the word *pretension* is the act of pretending.

Little girls love to pretend to be mommies. They play with their dolls and feed them imaginary milk from bottles. The little girls are not really mommies. It's all make-believe.

Little boys pretend to be Superman. They wear little capes their parents buy them. The truth is that it's pretend. They can't actually fly. It's not real!

Like these children, we know the difference between make-believe and reality. You enter a movie theater to see a "fantasy." You are watching imaginary characters. They are inventions of the writers, directors, and actors. They are not real people but fictional portrayals.

Just because they are not real, however, does not mean that your emotions are not moved. When the psychopathic killer, Freddy Krueger, swings his razor-sharp glove at a victim, the audience screams. We feel the terror on the screen. When Indiana Jones dangles over a deep gorge, our hearts race as we wonder how he will ever get out of this one. Even though we know it is a movie—a fantasy—we still feel fear and excitement. We are not, however, really afraid of being slashed or falling in the gorge ourselves, because we are able to separate our emotions from our intellect.

Our minds are much like the movie screen. Movies, often filled with scenarios that terrify us, play in our minds. We need to realize that what is in the mind is only a "pretension." It is not real. Unfortunately, many people cannot differentiate between the pretension in their minds and the truth of God's Word. Their strong emotions lead them to believe that the pretension is true. But it is not!

Raul has been a great blessing to our church, but when I first met him, he was a nervous wreck. The enemy had planted a thought in his mind that if he held anyone's hand, it would curse that person, so he refused to ever hold hands

in prayer. I had spoken to him for some time about this lie. He nodded and agreed that it was foolish to think that his hands could possibly curse others. Despite his agreement with me, he still struggled with the thought. It was only by feeding continually on the Word, which increased his trust in God, that Raul was able to break free from this lie. Now he is one of the great prayer warriors of our church, holding hands

Almost all mental problems are a result of accepting as true something that is imaginary.

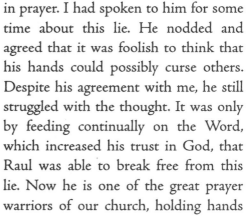

with anyone who will pray with him.

Mental Illness

One word describes the person who has a stronghold of pretension: *delusional.* This is a very strong word, but I want it to make an impact upon you. Almost all mental problems—from insanity to mild forms of compulsive behavior—are a result of accepting as true something that is imaginary.

The King James Bible uses the word *imaginations* instead of *pretension.* It means the same thing. There is something imaginary going on in the mind.

Through the years, I have had those in some sort of delusion argue with me, "You don't understand, Pastor. What I am feeling is really happening. I know you think I am crazy, but it's true; this is happening to me!" Then they will describe some outlandish incident they insist is happening to them.

As long as they argue against the truth, there is nothing anyone can do to help them. The pretension *"sets itself up against the knowledge of God"* (2 Corinthians 10:5). The phrase *"sets itself up"* carries the idea of "exaltation," as of an idol. An idol is unreal, like a thought; nevertheless, people bow to it as though it is the truth. In order for someone to be freed from his suffering, he must humble him or herself and admit that the pretension is a lie. But some are so prideful that they are convinced that what they believe is the truth.

In order for someone to be freed from his suffering, he must humble himself and admit that the pretension is a lie.

Rarely a week goes by that I do not have someone contacting me to share some delusional thought he has had. Let me tell you about four of the most common delusional thoughts I have heard through the years.

1. I have committed the unpardonable sin.

Rose and her husband had attended my church for a year. Three times, my wife and I had visited Rose at her request. She had been diagnosed with schizophrenia and was convinced that she had committed the "unpardonable sin." She told me that she had blasphemed the Holy Spirit, and she had read in the Bible that she could not be forgiven of such a sin.

I asked Rose, "Can you define for me the 'unpardonable sin'?"

She gave a blank stare and then tried to muster up a definition. "Uh, Pastor Brown, I have sex with demons, and this is unpardonable."

I shook my head, "Rose, this is not the unpardonable sin. What you are describing is something gross, but it is not blasphemy against the Spirit."

I proceeded to explain to Rose that demons cannot have sex with others because they do not have bodies. I opened up the Word and explained that she had *not* committed an unpardonable sin.

"Rose, first of all, if you had committed an unpardonable sin, you would have a hard heart and not be worried over it. Those who commit the unpardonable sin do not even think about it. The fact that you are worried about committing this sin is proof that you have not done it."

Rose shook her head. "I would like to believe you, but I know I have committed this sin, and God cannot forgive me."

Despite all my biblical arguments, I could not persuade Rose to believe the Word. She was determined to believe what she wanted. Peace could come to her only if she were able to trust in God. (See Isaiah 26:3.)

Rose and her husband eventually left my church and I lost contact with them for several years. Word eventually came to me that Rose had jumped in front of a train and killed herself.

I know this is a tragic story. I even hesitated to share it, but I realize that hope must be based on the truth. This tragic story is meant to shock you into the realization that even a minister cannot help someone who pridefully holds on to a lie.

Jesus sometimes used tragic stories to make an impression upon his listeners. He told of the rich man and Lazarus. The rich man's tragic story of burning in hell was meant to convey to the crowd the need to listen to the Scriptures. Jesus also told the story of a farmer who started with a happy life by having a bumper crop, but the story ends tragically with God saying, "*You fool! This very night your life will be demanded from you*" (Luke 12:20). Not a happy ending, is it?

Sometimes we learn more from tragic endings than from happy ones. I hope you can understand that arguing and exalting your own thoughts above God's will never lead to a sound mind.

2. I have demons that won't leave.

Diane had heard that MSNBC was coming to my church to tape a deliverance service. She told me that she needed deliverance, and she asked if she could be part of the documentary and have me drive the demons out of her.

I asked, "Diane, how do you know you have demons?"

"I have heard them speak through me."

"Do you have a pastor who knows you?"

"Yes."

"Has he ever prayed for you to be delivered?"

"Well, yes, he did years ago, but I still hear the voices. And now he tells me that he does not think I have demons."

"Diane, if he drove out the demons from you, how can you still hear the voices of demons?"

"I don't know, but I still do."

"Well, maybe the voices you hear are not demons. If they are not demons, there is no possibility that your pastor or I will be able to drive out what is not there."

"Pastor Brown, they will speak through me if you tell them to speak up."

I began to pray for Diane, and, sure enough, a voice came out of her mouth, saying, "You cannot cast me out. I belong here."

I questioned the voice, "Who is Jesus Christ?"

"Oh, he is a wonderful Savior, and I am afraid of him." In order to make sure it was a demon speaking and not Diane, I tried everything to get this supposed demon to curse Christ, but it would not. I realized that there were no demons talking through Diane, because the voice was so kind when it spoke of Christ. The voice's personality was Diane's.

"Diane, this is not a demon speaking through you."

"It's not?"

"No. A demon would never praise our Lord. It's clear that these words are from *you* and not a demon, because in your heart you love the Lord and could not make yourself curse Him."

Diane paused for a moment, "You are right. I could not say anything bad about Christ."

After conversing with me for awhile, she said, "I am so glad I have spoken to you. I always thought that a demon was inside me and no one could ever drive it out."

There are others like Diane. They honestly believe they have a demon that no one can cast out. The Word of God, however, says that Jesus gave us the *"authority to drive out all demons"* (Luke 9:1), and nothing can stand against us.

Occasionally, after I have prayed for deliverance over someone, that person will tell me, "The demon is still there. You did not cast it out."

I usually ask him, "Am I the first to ever attempt to drive out the demon?"

Almost always, he replies, "No, I have had many people try to drive out the demon. I have had the best and most famous ministers undertake to drive out this spirit, but no one can do it."

This is when I spell out the problem. "Do you know why no one can drive out a demon from you?"

"Why?"

"They can't drive out the demon because there is no demon to drive out." I explain, "There is a lying thought that was planted by the devil long ago. And the thought was, *I have a demon that is much too strong for anyone to cast out.* There is no demon in you, but only a thought. And no one has the power to cast out your thoughts. Only you can take authority and cast down your thoughts."

The Bible says we can *"cast down"* (2 Corinthians 10:5 KJV) imaginations and pretensions. There is a difference between casting *down* thoughts and trying in vain to cast them *out*. Thoughts cannot be *cast out*, but only *cast down*. The only people who can do that are the people who think the thoughts.

Some people have been told that they have demons. Usually it is a deliverance minister who fails to maintain a balance between the need to be delivered and the need for each person to take control over his own mind. These people are told by inexperienced ministers, "You have a demon, and it is going to take a long time before you can be set free."

These suggestive thoughts take the individual captive. That individual then begins to manifest what is expected of him. He may scream, feign voices, and manifest weird behavior, but the truth is that he simply has a thought in his mind planted by someone convincing him that he has demons.

Psychiatrists testified that when the movie *The Exorcist* came out in the 1970s, many of their patients began to exhibit a type of demonic possession that was depicted in the movie. While it may be true that the movie opened the dialogue for patients to question their psychiatric problems, and while some may have come to understand that their problems were legitimately the work of demons, I think the majority of cases were simply people allowing the movie to put the idea into their minds that they had demons.

Some will ask, "How do I know if there is a demon or not?" If no anointed person can cast out the demon, it is normally evidence that there is no demon. I realize that some demons do not come out except by prayer and fasting; however, after everything has been tried, there should come a time when a person realizes that he has received adequate prayer. At such a point, it must be understood that there are no demons. The person must recognize that *"the one who is in you is greater than the one who is in the world"* (1 John 4:4).

There are some whose minds are stayed on the devil. They actually believe the demons in them are greater than the Holy Spirit within them.

Perfect peace comes because your *"mind is stayed on* [God]" (Isaiah 26:3 KJV). There are some whose minds are stayed on the devil. They actually believe the demons in them are greater than the Holy Spirit within them. If they continue to exalt the devil over God, then they will continue to struggle with fear.

3. I have no hope to continue living.

For years, Michelle had put up with chronic illness and an unhappy marriage that had plunged her into depression. Convinced she would never again experience happiness, she began contemplating suicide. Fortunately, Michelle came to my Internet site and read all my materials. She read what I wrote about suicide and the need to fear the Lord. I showed her that God had a wonderful plan for her life. She began to see that she could be healed and experience joy again. She decided to give up her thoughts of suicide and trust God. When she did, hope sprung up in her heart. She wrote to me, saying, "For the first time in over a year, I want to live."

Hopelessness is one of Satan's greatest tools. This is why Paul wrote, *"Putting on faith and love as a breastplate, and the hope of salvation as a helmet"* (1 Thessalonians 5:8). A helmet covers the head, our minds. The devil cannot permanently injure our minds when we have them covered with the *"hope of salvation."* Hope is an expectation that everything will turn out for the best. Hope is not a fantasy, because God promised that *"in all things God works for the good of those who love him"* (Romans 8:28). A Christian who feels no hope is actually having a delusional thought. How can we who know the Lord not have hope?

A Christian who feels no hope is having a delusional thought.

May the God of hope fill you with all joy and peace as you trust in him, so that you may overflow with hope by the power of the Holy Spirit.

(Romans 15:13)

You might know Him as a God of love, but He is also a God of hope. You can *"overflow with hope"* if you *"trust in him."* If you are not overflowing with hope, it is a sure sign that you are not trusting in the Lord. It's time for you to put your trust in God, and He will cause everything to turn out for the best for you.

We know that in all things God works for the good of those who love him, who have been called according to his purpose. (Romans 8:28)

Cast all your anxiety on him because he cares for you. (1 Peter 5:7)

4. I can't forgive.

Pastor Albert experienced burnout. His right-hand man left, taking nearly one-third of the congregation away to start a new church. Albert was embittered against his old friend. *How could he do this do me?* he thought.

I was invited by Pastor Albert to hold a series of meetings at his church. It was the last night of the seminar when I felt led by the Lord to teach on forgiveness. I knew nothing of what was going on with him, but when I gave the call for people to forgive, Pastor Albert came forward, sobbing uncontrollably. The members who knew the situation gathered around and started to pray for him. From his heart, Albert totally forgave the man. In the end, he could sincerely wish the man all the best.

Albert told me that for the first time since the incident with that man, he was happy to be pastoring. On top of this, Albert realized that he had not been himself lately; he was preaching harshly, subconsciously taking out his frustration on the church. After he forgave, his sweet spirit returned. His congregation immediately noticed a positive change in him. As a result of the change, his congregation grew rapidly and surpassed its size before the split.

People get the wrong idea that forgiveness is for the benefit of the offender. It's not. It is primarily for the benefit of the victim. Many people live in delusion, thinking that by holding a grudge, they are punishing the one who wronged them. In fact, they are mostly hurting themselves.

Pastor Joel Osteen recently recalled sitting in the backseat of the family car as a little boy with his father and

People get the wrong idea that forgiveness is for the benefit of the offender. It's not. It is primarily for the benefit of the victim.

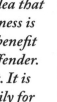

another man in the front. As the driver turned down a road, Joel's father, John, said, "Hey, brother, you're taking the long way. You should go straight."

The man replied, "Oh, I don't ever travel down that part of the road because 'so-and-so' lives there, and he did me wrong." Even though Joel was just a kid, he thought, *so-and-so does not even know that this man avoids him. He probably couldn't care less, yet this man goes out of his way to avoid him.*

How many of us are like this man? Do we actually think the people who offended us are hurt by our not forgiving them? Can you see the delusional reasoning? When you hold grudges against others, they actually hold power over you. Forgiving other people actually frees you from their power, and this is the ultimate way to liberate yourself from the hurt.

Chapter Fifteen

How to Get Your Mind Back

The weapons we fight with are not the weapons of the world. On the contrary, they have divine power to demolish strongholds.   (2 Corinthians 10:4)

What should you do to get rid of the strongholds in your mind? *Stronghold* comes from a word meaning "fortress." A fortress is a place of security. In this case, your thoughts can give Satan a secure place in which to work his plot in your life. It is a place where Satan has a defense, a protected position.

You may have visited some of the sites of historic forts built around the world. They usually have high walls surrounding other buildings. How do you destroy a fort? One way is with a wrecking ball. You can't just hope the walls fall down; you must force them down. This is true with your mind as well. You cannot continue to hope that your mind will get back to normal. You will have to fight for it.

1. Recognize that nothing is greater than God.

We "*have divine power to demolish strongholds.*" Satan has power, but not "*divine power.*" You must understand that it will take divine power to destroy and demolish the strongholds in your mind.

God's power is greater than demonic power.

God's mercy is greater than sin.

God love in your heart is greater than the bitterness you feel.

God's healing power is greater than disease.

God's provision is greater than lack.

God's wisdom is greater than confusion.

If you think your problem is greater than God's ability to solve it, then you will be overcome by fear. A person who believes his problem is greater than God is actually under a delusion. Nothing is higher than God.

If you think your problem is greater than God's ability to solve, then you will be overcome by fear.

Liesl Alexander was diagnosed with severe mental illness and hospitalized by a court order. No one blamed her for her condition. After all, she grew up with alcoholic parents and a distant father. Her dysfunctional family situation was further complicated by a blind grandmother, a neurotic great-aunt, and a twin sister with a similar illness. Liesl had all the genetic makings for a lifetime spent in mental health institutions.

In desperation, she tried everything to get her mind back. She delved deeply into the occult, trying to find answers for her messed-up life, but it did not bring her a sound mind.

One day a few Christians visited her. She was surprised to feel a sense of peace as they talked to her about Jesus. They calmly told Liesl of God's love for her and explained that He could heal her mind.

What? These words seem too good to be true. The Christians gathered in a circle around her, laid their hands on her, and spoke a simple prayer: "Lord Jesus, please heal this girl's mind."

Suddenly a "click" went off in Liesl's head. She came face-to-face with a light that totally enveloped her. She became completely aware of the presence of Jesus. For the first time, she had hope that she would be normal. After the visitors left, Liesl felt better but knew something was still missing. At three o'clock in the morning, she surrendered her life to Christ. Through her tears, she prayed, "I believe in You, Jesus. I want to follow You. Please come into my life and put right whatever is wrong." Suddenly, she was overwhelmed by an awareness of God's power and goodness.

Since that encounter, Liesl has been totally healed and was delivered from the severe mental illness that doctors believed would never be cured. She is now married to an Anglican vicar, and she travels around sharing her testimony. Liesl has come to realize that there is no mental illness beyond God's ability to cure.

2. Uncover each lie you have believed and search Scripture to prove it wrong.

We take captive every thought to make it obedient to Christ.   (2 Corinthians 10:5)

If we allow even one lie to continue to work freely in our minds, it will continue to bring us trouble.

There can be no enemies left lurking in the darkness when an army overtakes a fort. They will only bring needless injuries to the army trying to secure the stronghold. Every member of the enemy that remains must be taken captive. The same is true with every lie we have accepted as truth. We must imprison every lie that once imprisoned us. If we allow even one lie to continue to work freely in our minds, it will continue to bring us trouble.

What are the lies you have believed? You need to replace them with the truth, but you must have Scripture to back it up. Some may say, "I don't have time to look up verses." That's a lie. You have time to sit for an hour telling your problems to a counselor. You have time to sit for hours waiting for your doctor appointment. You even have time to sit in front of the television.

We all have time. It's a matter of prioritizing the time we have. What is important to you? You must get into the Word of God to find the truth so that you can use it to destroy the lies that have besieged your mind.

3. Speak the Word of God to the stronghold, because God releases His power through your lips.

> *The weapons we fight with are not the weapons of the world.* (2 Corinthians 10:4)

The apostle Paul listed the armor of God in Ephesians 6. A close look at the armor, however, reveals that there is only one offensive weapon mentioned: the sword of the Spirit—the spoken Word of God. (See Ephesians 6:17.) If you have the Word of God only in your head and it never comes out of your mouth, it is as though you have a sword that you leave in its sheath. You must pull it out and use it by actually speaking the Word of God. Words are greater than thoughts. A thought is powerful, but words are more dominant. God's Word, when spoken out loud to yourself while you read Scripture, is a good way to bring your thoughts under control.

To actually rebuke Satan, you must quote Bible verses, not merely say "I rebuke you" over and over.

Jesus knew this. When He was tempted with wrong thoughts, He spoke out loud to the devil, *"It is written"* (Matthew 4:4, 7, 10). Though armed with Scripture, even Jesus could not overcome Satan simply with His thoughts or His *mind*, but only with the Word in His *mouth*. Take the verses you have learned and speak them aloud until the stronghold is broken.

This is not the same as screaming at the top of your voice, repeating the overly used phrase, "I rebuke you, Satan!" Saying "I rebuke you" is not really rebuking Satan. *Rebuke* is a verb. *To rebuke* is to do something about Satan. To actually rebuke Satan, you must quote Bible verses against him, not merely say "I rebuke you" over and over. To repeat this empowers Satan in your life, because your thoughts are focused on him and not on God's promises. It is best to simply take specific Bible passages and quote them out loud.

Make a list. On one side, write down the problem areas in your life. In the next column, find passages that address those areas.

Example

Problem Areas	Scripture Passages
Sexual lusts	Job 31:1; Romans 6:1–7; Colossians 3:5; 1 Thessalonians 4:4

Pray out loud, using these passages, to destroy that stronghold in your mind. In the example above, the prayer might go something like this:

> Father God, *"I make a covenant with my eyes not to look lustfully at a girl"* (Job 31:1). I will not go on sinning so grace may increase. I died to sin and cannot live in it any longer. I was buried with Christ through baptism, into death, so that, just as Christ was raised from the dead through the glory of the Father, I, too, may live a new life. My old self has been crucified with Christ, so that the body of sin might be done away with, that I will no longer be a slave to sin. (Romans 6:1–7.) I have died with Christ, and dead men do not sin. I *"put to death...whatever belongs to* [my] *earthly nature."* I put to death all *"sexual immorality, impurity, lust,* [and] *evil desires"*

(Colossians 3:5). I will *"learn to control* [my] *own body in a way that is holy and honorable"* (1 Thessalonians 4:4).

You can make God's Word your prayer with every problem area of your life. There is hardly a day in our ministry that someone does not tell us of some major mental problem in his life that he attributes to demons. Some indeed do have demons, so I offer to pray the prayer of deliverance for them. In the majority of cases, however, I find no demonic indwelling, but simply lies that people have believed as truth. Many of them have received many prayers for deliverance, yet they do not improve; they get worse. It's clear the problem is in their minds.

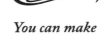

You can make God's Word your prayer with every problem area of your life.

The four delusional lies in the previous chapter were included because they are the ones that most mentally ill people have accepted as truth. Thus, I have incorporated a powerful Scripture-based prayer that will destroy these specific strongholds of the mind. If you find yourself struggling with any of these issues, I want you to look up the passage provided and pray the prayer. Do not for a moment continue to accept such delusional thoughts as truth. It is time to move forward and claim the victory that is yours.

Problem Areas	Scripture Passages
Guilt	Psalm 103:2–12; Romans 8:1; John 14:16

214 ～ Devil, Demons, and Spiritual Warfare

Problem Areas	Scripture Passages
Demons	1 John 4:4; James 4:7; Mark 16:17; Luke 10:19
Suicidal Thoughts	Jeremiah 29:11; Psalm 118:17; Nehemiah 8:10; Isaiah 12:3
Unforgiveness	Romans 5:5; Ephesians 4:32; Job 5:2; Matthew 7:1–5; 18:21–35

Guilt

Father God, I come in the name of Jesus. I recognize that the devil has deceived me by making me think that I have committed an unpardonable sin. You, however, have promised to forgive *all* my sins. As far as the east is from the west, this is how far You have removed my sin from me. (Psalm 103:12.) Thank You for forgiving me. There is now no condemnation for me, because I am in Christ Jesus. (Romans 8:1.) The Holy Spirit has never left me, because Jesus promised that He would remain with me forever. (John 14:16.)

Demons

Demons have lied to me and caused me to think that they would never leave me. But I recognize that the Holy Spirit within me is greater than any demons in the world. (1 John 4:4.) Whom the Son sets free is free indeed. Demons are in the world, but they do not dwell in me. I am free from every demon. I can even resist the devil, who runs from me in stark terror. (James 4:7.) The devil and demons are afraid of me. I am the one who can cast them out. I have authority in the name of Jesus to drive out all demons. (Mark 16:17.) I have been given authority over all the power of the enemy, and nothing shall harm me. (Luke 10:19.)

Suicidal Thoughts

I reject any thoughts of suicide. There is no need to dwell on death when God has promised me a great future. He has planned to bless me and give me hope and a fabulous destiny. (Jeremiah 19:11.) *"I will not die but live, and will proclaim what the Lord has done"* (Psalm 118:17). *"The joy of the Lord is* [my] *strength"* (Nehemiah 8:10), and *"with joy* [I] *will draw…from the wells of salvation"* (Isaiah 12:3). I have hope that I will find love, that I will be healed, and that my finances will turn for the better. I trust in the God of hope.

Unforgiveness

God has poured His love into my heart (Romans 5:5) by the Holy Spirit, so I can love and forgive anyone just as God has forgiven me. (Ephesians 4:32.) I will be wise and let go of resentment. I

216 ~ Devil, Demons, and Spiritual Warfare

will stop holding grudges against others. I will not look to judge them or find fault with them. I get out of my inner prison by forgiving anyone who has harmed me. I have a sound mind!

When you make these claims in prayer, the imaginary thoughts, which have been deeply rooted, will fight against the truth you are praying. Do not give in to these thoughts and quit praying. Instead, keep praying these prayers over your life until the stronghold is demolished. Your words are like a wrecking ball, and sometimes you have to keep hitting the stronghold until it collapses. Do not stop praying until you see victory. Increase your knowledge of Scripture by adding your own verses and personal prayers. How will you know it is working? The stronghold has been destroyed when you feel peace. Peace comes when the war ends. It is a great feeling.

> *The stronghold has been destroyed when you feel peace. Peace comes when the war ends. It is a great feeling.*

Don't become complacent. Even after the stronghold is down, it is a good idea to continue to speak those passages as preventive medicine to keep it from ever being built again. In the same way that taking vitamin C will build your immunity when you are healthy, Scripture will guard your heart and mind against Satan's future assaults.

Julie came to my church for the first time with deep depression and suicidal thoughts. She was a single mother, her relationship with her boyfriend was over, she had lost all hope of a better life, and she felt that God had abandoned her. She was a nervous wreck. Julie did not know what to expect at our church, but she accepted Christ that night. For the first time in a long time, a gleam of hope penetrated the darkness of her bleak world. Her problems did not end immediately, but as she faithfully pursued God at our church, her thinking began to straighten out. Through biblical teaching, she learned how to pray the right prayers over her life. In a short time, her depression was completely gone. Since then, Julie has married a wonderful, God-fearing man, and she now leads our prayer ministry and is our youth pastor. She has come a long way, and so can you!

In all my years of ministry, I have never seen a person who has practiced these three steps fail to demolish the stronghold in his mind.

Chapter Sixteen

Satan's Final Judgment

A little girl came to me with a grave look. Her inquisitive, brown eyes showed the seriousness of her question: "Pastor Brown, why didn't God just kill the devil?"

Though her question brought a smile, I realized how her question hit the heart of the matter concerning spiritual warfare. Nearly everyone wonders: *Why did God leave the devil here to give us problems?* God understands our difficult situation, so how can we enjoy true fellowship with Him while the devil is constantly attacking us?

It is not God's ultimate, eternal will for us to engage in spiritual warfare. To that end, He has planned "The Day" for Satan, demons, and fallen angels to be eternally judged and removed from any influence upon our lives. Demons recognize this truth, for they once shouted at Christ, *"Have you come here to torture us before the appointed time?"* (Matthew 8:29). They know there is an appointed time for their eternal judgment.

Satan also knows that the time is coming when he will no longer be able to deceive the nations. Revelation 20:2–3 says,

> *He seized the dragon, that ancient serpent, who is the devil, or Satan, and bound him for a thousand years. He threw him into the Abyss, and locked and sealed it over him, to keep him from deceiving the nations anymore until the thousand years were ended. After that, he must be set free for a short time.*

After the thousand years are over,

> *The devil, who deceived them, was thrown into the lake of burning sulfur, where the beast and the false prophet had been thrown. They will be tormented day and night for ever and ever.*

> (Revelation 20:10)

This is Satan's final and eternal judgment! Never again will he and his fallen angels be allowed to deceive the world.

God's intention is for Satan to remain here until we complete our earthly mission. His judgment, therefore, is linked to our faithfulness.

We will live in eternal bliss—paradise, no warfare.

"The Day" has not yet arrived.

It is interesting to note that on the same day that Satan is cast into the lake of fire, the whole earth will be judged. (See verse 12.) This means that the day of judgment will be for the world, as well as for Satan. God's intention is for Satan to remain here until we complete our earthly mission. His judgment, therefore, is linked to our faithfulness to God.

Since God is good, He cannot tempt us. "*When tempted, no one should say, 'God is tempting me.' For God cannot be tempted by evil, nor does he tempt anyone*" (James 1:13).

In the garden of Eden, it was Satan, not God who suggested that Adam and Eve eat the forbidden fruit. It is he who brings the tests and temptations of life. I believe that God allows Satan to test us. We cannot face judgment until we have faced the tests that prove our faithfulness to God. In His wisdom, God allowed Satan to remain here for the purpose of our testing and sanctification.

The School of Spiritual Warfare

These are the nations the LORD left to test all those Israelites who had not experienced any of the wars in Canaan (he did this only to teach warfare to the descendants of the Israelites who had not had previous battle experience). (Judges 3:1–2)

God left enemies on the earth in order to teach warfare to Israel. They had to learn the ways of courage, answer the call of duty, be skilled in weaponry, risk their lives in battle, and depend on God's power for their victory. As with Israel, God left the devil here with all of his cohorts in order for believers to learn the ways of spiritual warfare. While we should try to avoid *natural* warfare whenever possible, we can learn something from *spiritual* warfare.

You might argue, "Why do I need to learn warfare?" Let me give you seven lessons that spiritual warfare will teach you.

1. It teaches you to take sides.

After 9/11, President George Bush told the world, "You are either with us, or you are with the terrorists." A line was drawn in the sand. Of course, you can't draw a line if there is no opposition. Without the devil, you would not have a choice. By allowing the devil to be here, God gives mankind a choice. "You are either with Me, or you are with the devil."

God does not want anyone worshipping Him by default. He does not want worship unless you *choose* to worship Him. There is no choice when there is only one option.

God does not want anyone worshipping Him by default. He does not want worship unless you choose to worship Him.

In March 2008, Russia elected Dmitry Medvedev as its new president. This was no true election by any account. He was the only viable name on the ballot. For there to be a true election, people must have legitimate choices. Elections are a sham when voters have no choices. Even when the people make the wrong choice, it is a choice nevertheless.

God took a risk by allowing the devil to tempt the first couple and, later, the rest of humanity. The fact that so many have chosen to follow the devil is proof that God allowed a legitimate choice to tempt us. As we begin to engage in spiritual warfare, we are confronted with a choice—there is a need to take sides. Are we going to side in with the devil, or with God?

During the Civil War, President Abraham Lincoln was asked if he thought God was on his side. He wisely replied,

"It is not is God on my side, but am I on God's side?" This is the question spiritual warfare answers for us.

2. It teaches you through your mistakes.

"These are the nations the LORD *left to test all"* (Judges 3:1). In spiritual warfare, we face tests. There are times when we may lose the battle for a short season. It has been said, "You learn more from defeat than you do from victory." You learn through mistakes. After taking a test and receiving the results, what do you notice more than anything? You notice the red marks highlighting all of your mistakes. You are drawn immediately to your wrong answers more than to the right ones. This is what spiritual warfare will teach you.

Tests reveal what you really know.

I took the Federal Aviation Administration (FAA) pilot test and passed. In preparation for the test, I took a course taught on DVD. Although I learned a lot from the lectures, the most helpful part of the course was taking the many sample tests. Questions were asked, and I would click on my answers. As I went back over the corrected test, the wrong answers made a greater impact on my learning than the right ones. I never gave an incorrect answer to any question more than once. When I went back and listened to the same lectures, I was able to comprehend so much more. The only way I came to learn more was by taking the tests.

The same is true of spiritual warfare. It is the test we take. After finally passing the tests and winning the victory, we can go back to the Word of God and listen once more to His teaching, and we comprehend so much more because of the test we took. It will really teach you what is in your heart.

3. It teaches you to become grateful and humble.

> *The* LORD *your God will drive out those nations before you, little by little. You will not be allowed to eliminate them all at once, or the wild animals will multiply around you.* (Deuteronomy 7:22)

The Israelites did not enjoy entering into a Promised Land that was teeming with enemies. In the same way, we may not enjoy entering into our salvation while still having to face the enemies of the spirit. God, however, reveals the benefits of allowing our enemies to remain in the land by suggesting that they will keep the wild animals from multiplying.

If we did not have to fight the devil, then we would face deeper and more dangerous problems, such as pride, laziness, indifference, greed, and a host of other fleshly sins.

If we did not have to fight the devil, then we would face deeper and more dangerous problems, such as pride, laziness, indifference, greed, and a host of other fleshly sins. Peacetime will cause an army to become soft and flabby. Spiritual warfare causes us to be more vigilant. It will make us humble ourselves before God as we face our spiritual enemies.

Warfare becomes a sifting process just as it was for Peter when the devil asked Jesus if he could sift Peter *"as wheat"* (Luke 22:31). You cannot eat chaff, so it must be "sifted" from the rest of the wheat. So it is with our lives. We have ugly things in our hearts that only spiritual warfare can drive away. Without difficulties, we would become prideful, arrogant, and lacking compassion for others. Facing spiritual testing humbles us. God knows how much victory we can stand before it actually harms us.

4. It teaches you to appreciate the sufferings of your Lord.

> *Your enemy the devil prowls around like a roaring lion looking for someone to devour. Resist him, standing firm in the faith, because you know that your brothers throughout the world are undergoing the same kind of sufferings.*　(1 Peter 5:8–9)

One word describes the effect of spiritual warfare: suffering.

The people who most appreciate the suffering of the military are those who serve in the military. There is camaraderie and incredible commitment among soldiers. Likewise, when we go through spiritual warfare and experience the suffering that goes with it, we more fully appreciate the suffering that Christ went through.

Valuing His suffering will give you the courage to fight. It will give you the backbone to sacrifice for the sake of the gospel. The places that experience great revival are also the places that experience great spiritual conflict. Perhaps this is why the churches in the world experiencing the greatest persecution for their faith are also experiencing the greatest growth and miraculous provision. We hear their stories and wonder, in our relative safety, whether we, too, would be able to stand up against such oppression. Their courage is the direct result of their appreciation of the sufferings of Christ.

5. It teaches you to depend on God and not yourself.

> *Indeed, in our hearts we felt the sentence of death. But this happened that we might not rely on ourselves but on God, who raises the dead.*
>
> (2 Corinthians 1:9)

> *Finally, be strong in the Lord and in his mighty power.* (Ephesians 6:10)

Far too often, we deceive ourselves into thinking that we have the natural ability to deal with any issue, only to

It is imperative that we depend on God to overcome the devil, because there is no natural power that will defeat him.

realize that the problems we face are far greater than our human abilities. In our desperation, we finally look to God's power for the answer. Spiritual warfare will teach you to trust in God and not in yourself.

We don't want to be strong in ourselves but in the Lord and in His mighty power. It is imperative that we depend on God to overcome the devil, because there is no natural power that will defeat him.

A photographer was ordered by his newspaper to take pictures of raging wildfires in southern California. He was told that a small plane would be waiting for him at the airport. When he arrived at the airport, he saw a man standing by a plane, so he jumped in, saying, "Hurry up, we're late!" At an altitude of about five thousand feet, the photographer told the pilot to take him closer to the flames.

"Isn't that a little dangerous?" the pilot replied.

"C'mon man, you can do it," said the photographer, taking out his camera.

The pilot looked at the camera in the photographer's hand and asked, "Hey, you are my instructor, aren't you?"

Spiritual warfare is no laughing matter. When you are in the pilot's seat, you better be depending on God and not on yourself.

6. It teaches you that God is proud of you.

The devil constantly accused Job of lacking character. But after Job faithfully went through every trial, it showed the devil how proud God was of Job. God said to Satan, *"Have you considered my servant Job?"* (See Job 1:8, 2:3.) God loves to brag about His children to Satan.

Nothing brings more pride to a father than seeing his children overcome an opponent, whether it is during a sporting event, a spelling bee, or any kind of contest. When I was eleven, my baseball coach called me to relieve the starting pitcher during a game. The bases were loaded, there were two outs, and we were winning by one run. I struck out the batter, and we won the game! The coach wrapped an arm around me, looked at my father, and said, "Tommy won it for us today." I still remember the smile on my father's face. He was grinning from ear to ear. This is the way God feels when we overcome the devil.

7. It teaches you personal victory.

> *The God of peace will soon crush Satan under your feet.* (Romans 16:20)

God does not crush Satan with His feet, but with *your* feet. Watching a game is exciting, but playing in it is far more rewarding. If God had removed Satan from our midst, then we would never enjoy the feeling of putting him under our feet. One of the reasons God allows him to remain is to give us the feeling of victory when we defeat him.

God does not crush Satan with His feet, but with your feet.

The seventy-two disciples were thrilled when they saw that demons submitted to them in Jesus' name. (See Luke 10:17.) There is no spiritual adventure you can appreciate more than watching the devil and his demons flee. God wants to share with us in our victory over the devil by allowing us to punish him with our God-given authority.

Justin had always wanted a tree house, so he pleaded with his father to build one. His father agreed and began work on it. Justin watched from his window as his father went to work. After two weeks, it was done.

In another family, Caleb also wanted a tree house. His father also agreed to build it, but only *with* Caleb's help. Together they gathered the materials, took turns sawing, and alternated hammering the nails. After two weeks, the tree house was completed.

Which of the boys do you suppose appreciated the tree house more? Certainly, it was Caleb, who built the structure together with his father. He felt a sense of accomplishment. This is exactly what God wants us to feel. He could have defeated the devil alone, without our participation; instead, He prefers it when we help to finish the job of defeating the devil.

Paradise

As you ponder the thoughts and ideas in this book, you may find yourself with more questions still unanswered. You may wonder if you will ever be able to overcome a particular situation.

Child of God, He is with you right now. There is no problem for which God has not already provided the solution. In your struggle against the spiritual forces of evil, you will learn a great deal about yourself and about God's love for you. In addition, you will experience a personal sense of victory when you win the spiritual battles in your life, with your Father's help.

Although spiritual warfare is not pleasant when you are in it, the victory is so sweet when it's over.

Although spiritual warfare is not pleasant when you are in it, the victory is so sweet when it's over. Take solace in the fact that we will not always be fighting a spiritual battle. The time is coming when Satan and all his forces will finally be judged forever. *"To him who overcomes, I will give the right to eat from the tree of life, which is in the paradise of God"* (Revelation 2:7). Your obligation is simple: to overcome. As a victor, you will look back in time and realize that all the struggle, all the effort, and all of the lessons learned were well worth it.

About the Author

Tom Brown is best known for his deliverance ministry. Millions have seen him on ABC's *20/20*, as well as on MSNBC and The History Channel. He is a noted conference speaker, prolific author, and committed pastor. His award-winning internet site, www.tbm.org, reaches more than a million people a year. Tom resides in El Paso, Texas with his beautiful wife and wonderful children.

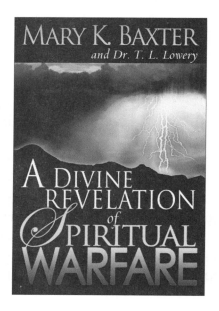

A Divine Revelation of Spiritual Warfare
Mary K. Baxter and Dr. T. L. Lowery

Best-selling author Mary K. Baxter reports from personal experience what it is like to be opposed by powerful, unseen spiritual enemies. She has learned the secrets of defeating both sin and Satan. In *A Divine Revelation of Spiritual Warfare*, you'll learn how to receive divine protection and use the spiritual weapons that are rightfully yours as a child of God. Find out how you can participate in Christ's victory over the enemy right now and live a victorious life!

ISBN: 978-0-88368-694-2 ◆ Trade ◆ 208 pages

WHITAKER
HOUSE

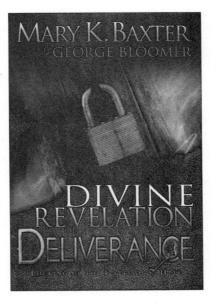

A Divine Revelation of Deliverance
Mary K. Baxter with George Bloomer

Many Christians live with frustration and defeat. They wonder why they can't overcome sins and temptations, even though they pray and try to be strong. Yet God loves us and wants to set us free. Through Christ, He gives us victory over the enemy and the power to deliver others who are pawns of Satan's destructive plans. Mary K. Baxter exposes Satan's schemes and provides much-needed hope for the suffering and oppressed. Receive a divine revelation of your deliverance in Christ!

ISBN: 978-0-88368-754-3 • Trade • 224 pages

WHITAKER
HOUSE

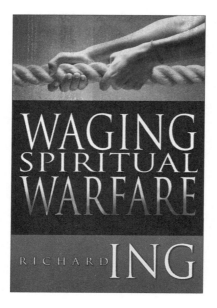

Waging Spiritual Warfare
Richard Ing

Dr. Richard Ing shares his extensive worldwide experience with unseen and powerful enemies. He exposes how to defeat the deceptions used by Satan whose plan is to destroy your spirit, soul, and body. Find out how to be equipped for spiritual battle and how to bring powerful angels to assist you, identify the enemy's strategies, break through strongholds, and minister to the oppressed. By exercising the authority that God has given you, you will discover that you can effectively block Satan's evil attacks and achieve victory.

ISBN: 978-1-60374-022-7 ✦ Trade ✦ 208 pages

WHITAKER
HOUSE

Identifying and Breaking Curses
John Eckhardt

Perhaps you are plagued by family disputes and bickering. Your marriage is crumbling and you just can't seem to connect with your kids. Maybe you're sick and living from paycheck to paycheck. You've prayed and prayed some more, but nothing seems to work. No matter what your ailment is— financial, familial, physical—you may unknowingly be living under a curse. John Eckhardt discusses how you can identify curses and break them, not only in your own life, but also in the lives of others.

ISBN: 978-0-88368-615-7 • Trade • 64 pages

WHITAKER
HOUSE

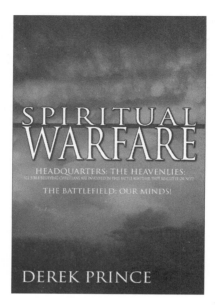

Spiritual Warfare
Derek Prince

Resist the enemy's attacks.
Tear down the enemy's strongholds.
Learn the key to victory.

Derek Prince explains the battle that's happening now between the forces of God and the forces of evil. Choose to be prepared by learning the enemy's strategies so you can effectively block his attacks. We have God on our side, and nothing will keep us from victory!

ISBN: 978-0-88368-670-6 • Trade • 144 pages

WHITAKER
HOUSE

Lucifer Exposed: The Devil's Plan to Destroy Your Life
Derek Prince

Satan, the fallen archangel, desires nothing more than to win the loyalty, hearts, and minds of the entire human race—and he won't quit in his attempt to win you over! Are you—or someone you know—struggling with abuse, pornography, addiction, gluttony, or other issues? Use the mighty spiritual weapons revealed in this compelling book, and victory can be yours!

ISBN: 978-0-88368-836-6 • Trade • 160 pages

WHITAKER
HOUSE

Strongman's His Name...What's His Game?
Drs. Jerry & Carol Robeson

Instead of "binding" symptoms, we can attack the sixteen strongmen or demonic spirits mentioned by name in the Bible. God names them, they are real, and He has given us dominion over them through the name of Jesus! Learn to instantly recognize when Satan is attacking and how to zero in on and quickly identify the strongman in every situation. Here is a scriptural, balanced, uplifting approach to present-day spiritual warfare.

ISBN: 978-0-88368-601-0 • Workbook • 180 pages

WHITAKER
HOUSE